BLOOD, SWEAT, GYPSIES AND DREAMS

by David J. Scott

Copyright 2013 by David J. Scott

All rights reserved. No part of this book may be reproduced in any form without written permission from the publisher.

In spite of my best efforts, the passage of time has made it nearly impossible to trace the origin of some of the photos, but a great many of them were given to us by many fans and supporters, and I thank them. Their donated and purchased photos help make this book possible.

Weekend Racer Publishing, LLC • 1201 Monument Blvd., Suite 14 • Concord, CA 94520 • U.S.A. • 925-332-8161

The opinions expressed in this manuscript are solely the opinions of the author and do not represent the opinions or thoughts of the publisher. The author has represented and warranted full ownership and/or legal right to publish all the materials in this book.

Blood, Sweat, Gypsies and Dreams
All Rights Reserved.
Copyright © 2014 David J. Scott
v2.0 R1.0

Cover Photo © 2014 David J. Scott. All rights reserved - used with permission.

This book may not be reproduced, transmitted, or stored in whole or in part by any means, including graphic, electronic, or mechanical without the express written consent of the publisher except in the case of brief quotations embodied in critical articles and reviews.

Outskirts Press, Inc.
http://www.outskirtspress.com

ISBN: 978-0-578-12576-3

Outskirts Press and the "OP" logo are trademarks belonging to Outskirts Press, Inc.

PRINTED IN THE UNITED STATES OF AMERICA

ACKNOWLEDGEMENTS

Neil Nicholson
Bill Boyd
Al Fergoda
Dudley Perkins Sr.
Harry Hunt
Bill Donnelly
Don Vesco
Lou and Al Geissler
Dick Lightner
Bob Fisher
Merv Wright
Dave Geddes
Sam Giammona
David Robb
Richard P. Allen D.D.S.
Alex Robles
Martin Marshall
Brian Mylchreest
David Mylchreest
Les and Joan Doherty
Patrick and Pooh Cowley
Bill and Jill Hamilton-Turner
The Caledonian Club
    of San Francisco
Floyd P. Busby
Jack Scott
Colin Scott
Dave Fender
Rolf and Gisella Korrmann
Tom Slappendell
Hagen Schultz
Rudy the Postman
Ian Newton
Jim Kelly
Bob Garrison
Paul and Debbie Stow
Alberto Xiol
Dani Agrati
Roberto Patrignani
Dr. Joe Ehrlich
Graham Duncan
Elspeth Spence
Rod Hurtado
Sue Oxendine
Billy Vassilou
Joe Olson

Contents..........

The Davie Scott Story: Scotland 1936-1985... 1
The Davie Scott Story: California...................... 18
EMC 1987: The Dr. Joe Ehrlich Saga ...56
Allan Scott Racing: The Privateers 1988 ..66
1989: The Year of Coronas 78
Garelli: The Last Factory Rider................... 102
Epilog.. 119

Thank You.......

A very special thank you to Jeff Markus, the Allan Scott Racing team mechanic, who stood by Allan loyally for four seasons, learning as he went, taking criticism from me from time to time, but enduring it. He was a vital part of our effort.

And of course my family, without their support none of this adventure could have taken place. I am especially grateful to my wife Jean, who stayed home, worried and worked hard to pay the mortgage and the bills, while Allan and I were abroad. She is a devoted mother and a very special lady.

Dave Scott Jr. kept us supplied with art work and T-shirts, and was our main liaison back in Califronia.

Hundreds of donors kept us racing. We thank them all for the support. You made it possible for our shoestring team to compete against the corporate sponsored teams. Your generosity was incredible. If I have missed someone, please forgive me!

A disappointing aspect of my racing career has been that the Glasgow Mercury Motorcycle Club has not recognized any of my contributions to the sport.

All through my years in racing, both in Scotland and America, I have proudly carried the Mercury badge on every helmet I have worn.

I was a member during the Bob McIntyre era, winning numerous races, and the Scottish Motor Racing Club Championship (200cc) in 1965, and claimed the Cooper Challenge Trophy that year. Alas you won't see my name on the Mercury Club's website history section?

Printed in the United States of America
Layout & Graphics by Floyd P. Busby

BLOOD, SWEAT, GYPSIES AND DREAMS

You may well be wondering why I chose this title?

There are two main characters in this story, who form the basis for the book, my son *Allan Scott* and myself, *Davie Scott*.

Both of us **BLED** profusely, at one time or another, during our separate careers, but kept on going regardless.

We also **SWEATED** like crazy, sometimes in sheer fear of the race ahead, but mostly just before the bills were due to be paid!

Why **GYPSIES**, you may ask?
We never considered ourselves to be Gypsies,
Travelers, Tinkers, Romany's or the like. We were just privateer racers, without whom there would have been no racing grid back in those days. But we were none the less, christened by Bernie Ecclestone, at a wet Belgian Grand Prix he promoted, and that designation remained with us for the duration!

The **DREAMS** part? This was the whole essence of my personal life story, and I passed it along to my son Allan. Can a human being truly live without dreaming?

I have attached a poem (author unknown), which I conspicuously posted in the library of our home in Pleasant Hill, California. The library was actually a bathroom, so everyone who visited the library could read the poem at their leisure, and perhaps become more motivated and inspired, *at least to simply keep on dreaming*. **Who could tell where a dream might lead to?**

David J. Scott

Dreams.....

Dreams have only one owner at a time.
That's why dreamers are lonely.
No one can help them with the struggle.
No one can ease the pain of failure.
There are some things they have to do themselves.
Winning is not what they're all about.
Neither are the rewards.
What is special about them is that they're dreamers who put it on the line.
They had the courage to admit that what they wanted was just beyond their reach,
    but if they wanted it badly enough, anything was possible.
They gambled. And for the risk, they were all rewarded with a legacy
    for others to follow.
For some it was a trail that was blazed, an attitude that was changed,
    a place in history, a thought, a life was touched.
That's the difference between them, and those who never take their dreams
    out of the box.
They leave nothing.

The Davie Scott Story
Scotland
1936 till 1967

I arrived on the scene on September 18th, 1936, the first born of Winston and Mary Scott, in the district of Milton, Glasgow, Scotland.

A quick glance at my birth certificate shows that I was delivered six months after my parents were married. In Scotland this situation is locally known as a "Hiv-tae Case" (Have to case). Here in America it is known as a "Shot Gun" marriage, so I was off to a great start. It would appear that I was an unfortunate accident, conceived in a heated moment of passion, in some dark alley or close.

Studying my Father as I grew up, it seemed unlikely to me that he ever loved my Mother.

It surely must have felt like the end of the world was nigh, to Winston and Mary, who were soon to become reluctant parents. The most shameful deed you could commit at that time in Scotland was to make a woman pregnant, out of wedlock, or it could be considered just slightly less heinous than murder!

At 18 months old, I was taken over by my Grandmother Francis Ferguson, and I never returned to my parent's miserable home until I was 16. While I was growing up, I made only infrequent short visits. I hated to visit that house, because it was inevitable that I would receive a verbal tongue lashing from my Dad, about being Grannie's wee boy!

My brother Jack was born 18 months after me, and he would remain with Mum and Dad. We knew we were brothers of course, but sadly we didn't get together too often.

World War Two was just starting when I turned four years of age, and I was off to school at this tender age, clutching my school bag and a gas mask!

There wasn't any kindergarten in Scotland back then. You had to hit the books at four, and didn't come up for air until you were 15!

My father was in the Royal Navy, and left the UK for service in the Indian Ocean. It would last four years, all of it spent in the Far East, until he returned for the Normandy invasion build up.

There was regular mail during his absence, so my brother and I knew what he looked like. Quite a good looking guy actually, resplendent in his Navy uniform.

My Mother was a striking woman, with jet black hair, a tiny person who looked almost Jewish. She also spent a lot of time in front of the mirror, and she was always fashion conscious, and immaculate.

"I was very fortunate to live with my Gran and Granda......"

I was very fortunate to live with my Gran and Granda, in their really nice house. It was not owned by them, but was in fact a company house.

Actually the whole family moved in to 10, Tyndrum Street for the duration of the war. The theory was that we should all be together if hit by a German bomb.

Granda was the caretaker of a large transport company called The Glasgow Hiring Company. The house overlooked a big garage and yard area, and the house came with the job.

Granda worked at the Glasgow Hiring Company, allowing us to live in a comforatable company-owned home.

My memories of the family during this period are fair, my Mother, Aunt Edith, Aunt Milly and Uncle Jack, were all single except for Mum.

The Americans were all over the place, as the build up for the invasion in Normandy developed, and as a result, the women folk were enamored and going crazy about the Yanks, including my own Mother and the Aunties. I was taking notice of everything now, as I was going to be eight soon.

She had dyed her jet black hair with peroxide by this time, as many others did before her. Scottish women thought they should all look like Betty Grable. I supposed it might increase their appeal to the Yanks!

My Granda Ferguson hated the Yanks. When he saw his daughters preparing to go dancing, and nylon hunting, he knew what was happening and despised them. I never knew what they did to get nylons of course, but I was already sensing that it was porobably not nice.

There were no nylon or silk stockings available for sale in the shops. Because of rationing it was impossible. The only alternative was to go bare legged, or apply leg tan which was made up by the local chemist.

I was a decent artist even at eight years of age, and I used to paint a thin black line down the back of each of their legs in simulation of real nylons. I often would see them when they returned home, leg tan all streaked and messy.

My 3-1/2 year old brother Jack, Judy and me at 5.

But the Yanks had plenty of real nylons, and women traded their bodies, and souls for them. I was certain that my Mother and Aunts were no exception. How else did they suddenly show up with nylons?

When my Father came home and saw the blonde hair, there was a tremendous fight, and nothing was ever the same with those two people. It was a dead marriage from there on in.

My Granda Ferguson passed away on January 29th, 1944 as the result of a cancerous tumor in his stomach. He was only 59, and I was just 8!

"We had to give up the house and were promptly scattered all over Glasgow......"

We had to give up the house and were promptly scattered all over Glasgow. I stayed on with my Gran of course, and my brother went with Mum and Dad.

The Aunts were beginning to marry and my Uncle Jack also took a wife. Life was about to get a lot tougher for me and Gran however, as we took a look at our next residence, which the company had found for Gran at 47 Raglan Street, near the Round Toll. Not a very good neighborhood, and the two room apartment was a dump!

The one room and kitchen was on the ground floor, no electricity or hot water. The coal burning range was the only source of heat, and to cook upon. The biggest shock however was the outside toilet, which had to be shared with two other families. We were in shock, but had no option, there was no alternative!

Lighting was by gas mantles, and power for the radio was by an accumulator, or battery, which had to be charged at a local store for a few pennies.

Poor Gran Ferguson, this was not the kind of living standard she was used to. I often heard her crying at night, which she firmly denied. Still, she soldiered on, and I truly loved her for her grit and determination. Thankfully I would inherit this trait from her. It would serve me well in years to come.

Gran had a serious addiction to snuff, which you may or may not know, is finely ground tobacco, it was almost the same as cocaine.

She was convinced that nobody knew about the snuff, and would swear me to secrecy when she sent me to the tobacconists for a quarter ounce of Irish snuff, her favorite.

She could never have concealed her habit completely, because she always left hankies lying around, which were stained brown from the snuff mucus. We all pretended that we did not notice this!

I often also surprised her when, in the freezing cold winters, she would be sitting up over the sink having a pee. Once again I just pretended that it never happened. I could never hurt or embarrass this fine lady.

Many nights we sat together, listening to the BBC on our battery powered radio, especially shows like ITMA (It's That Man Again) with Tommy Handley, the gas mantles hissing. It is impossible to forget those hard times.

She was living on a pension. My folks did not support me at all, and often we would be flat broke until her next pension payment. This meant that we had no single shilling coins for the gas meter, so we reverted to candles, and if the battery for the radio died, so be it….we read books by candlelight!

Now and then, we would also be out of food until pension day. If I was hungry, Gran would tell me to drink water. It tends to kill your yearning for food temporarily. Try it the next time you are hungry!

When we were flush she would always feed me a snack before bed, claiming that she did not want me to die of night starvation?

I stayed at my primary school on Milton Street for four more years until I was 12, as it was an easy walk from Raglan Street.

Now I was to attend St. George's Road Secondary High School. But more important to me, was that I was now eligible to work part-time. Imagine how I felt when I brought home my first pay packet to Gran?

After school I delivered groceries for a local grocer called Cochranes. They provided a special bike with a small front wheel to accommodate the big wicker basket in front of the handle bars. I believe this was my very first venture on two wheels. There would be many more adventures on two wheels in my future!

"…….I was working now and would never look back!"

Believe it or not, this somewhat meager extra income made a tremendous difference to me and Gran. I was working now and would never look back!

I did well in school, finishing first in class for two out of my three years. I slipped to third because I went to the potato harvest for a month, and I was being touted by my school masters to continue my education, possibly even make it into a college. All it took was money. I had to be realistic, it was not going to happen!

However, one thing I was absolutely sure would not happen. I would not be another unskilled laborer like my father, no sir, I was going to be an apprentice of some kind, somewhere. I just didn't know where it was going to be!

No one in my immediate family could advise me. It was all on me to find an apprenticeship. So off I went, interviewing without a clue.

I knew that I did not want to work in one of the many shipyards dotted along the River Clyde. This was heavy engineering, and it did not appeal to me. I luckily ended up signing on with L.Sterne and Company, Marine Refrigeration Engineers. I started work at 15 and experienced every aspect, and department of the company. My official apprenticeship would commence on September 18th 1952. This was my 16th birthday. If I completed my 5 year term, I would be classified as a Journeyman Tool and Die Maker. There would be no more laborers in my side of the Scott family!

I was by this time, quite a serious bicycle rider, but was about to buy a small motorized moped called an NSU Quickly.

My father had an old Norton ES2, but he would never dream of letting me ride the thing. All of my uncles on my dad's side had motor bikes as well, none of whom would let me ride either. I was on my own when it came to motorbikes!

One friend of the family, Maurice Mcgraw, did however let me ride his bike, and in years to come, I would inherit his helmet colors, black and white rings. Maurice had inherited these colors from an English factory scrambles rider named Bill Barugh.

I kept these colors throughout my career, as did my two sons when they raced. I never once had to ask someone not to copy me, but I was questioned by Albert Moule about the design. His was pale blue and black rings. He understood when I explained the lineage.

My brother Jack had told me that he and the parents were moving to a brand new flat in Drumchapel's number one scheme, and he thought that I should consider coming with Gran as well. It certainly would be nice to get out of the Raglan Street hovel.

The down side of this idea was that Gran and I would have to surrender our independence. We would be under the jurisdiction of Winston. There was room for us for sure, but would my Mum and Dad buy the program if we asked?

Jack said that the old man was always working. He was now a bus driver in the Glasgow Corporation Transport Authority, and grabbed all the overtime he could get. Jack said we would rarely cross paths.

Gran and I got the O.K to move in. Jack was right about the old man, I rarely saw him. My Mum was also a late person. She was the manager of a bar in Partick called The Windsor Tavern, and rarely got home before midnight.

Not long after Gran and I moved in, my parents had a real knock down, drag out fight, and the old man moved out. He went to my Granda Scott's house in Possilpark, where he was born and raised.

I never asked my Mum what it was all about, but I had a feeling that she was perhaps having an affair with someone from the bar, and my Dad had found out about it. This was pure speculation.

I could never agree to allow my wife, if I ever had one, to work in a bar. A woman would be pretty vulnerable and easily attracted to some sympathetic guy, especially if she was in a bad marriage, and I suspect that this is what happened.

On the evening of October 6th, 1954, Mum came home at about 11p.m.. I was still up, and had a short chat with her. She always changed into her under-slip before turning in for the night. She was wearing a black slip this night.

"At about 4a.m. my Gran came into my room and wakened me up. She said she could smell gas!"

At about 4a.m., my Gran came into my room and wakened me up. She said she could smell gas! I had a bad feeling right away, and it was confirmed when I opened the kitchen door. Mum had stuck her head in the gas oven and she was dead!

Lying there in her black slip, she was finally at peace, and free from this miserable marriage. She was just 38, and I had just turned 18 in September. What a tragedy!

The police and the coroner came and removed Mum. I said I would go to my Granda's house and tell my Dad. It was now 5.30am, and I hopped on my NSU to go break the news to Winston.
I had little to say to him, and he to me. This was a catastrophe. We would be hard pressed to recover from this, or restore any relationship that may have existed between us.

That night I swore I would get out of his house, and away from this man as soon as I could, and that I would someday start my own family, learning from the terrible job my father had made of his marriage. I swore I would never let this happen to me. I said to myself that it was time to look for a partner and begin a real life together.

Gran was devastated, and could barely look at Winston. She and him were at loggerheads all the time. I got on with my work and tried to forget.

It was 1955 now. A friend of mine, Tom McPherson, also had a made-in-Germany NSU Quickly, and I suggested that we ride them to Germany and visit the factory in Neckarsulm. He said let's do it, and I got a trip plan from the Royal Automobile Club. This would help me take my mind off of the death of Mum.

We would ride to Newcastle in the North East coast of England and board a ship to Esbjerg in Denmark. Bear in mind that these NSU's were powered by a tiny 50cc two stroke engine with pedal assistance if needed.

After a rough North Sea crossing, lasting 23 hours, we headed down through Denmark and crossed into Northern Germany, and on through the Schleswig-Holstein area to Hamburg. This was as far as we got before we started to run out of money. I decided that I was going to cross the English Channel instead of the North Sea. This way I would drop in on my Aunt Millie in Stroud, Gloucestershire, and borrow some money to get home.

23 hours on the North Sea to Denmark.

Tom said he was going to retrace his steps and return to Newcastle, so we went our separate ways, and that was that. We both made it home to Glasgow with saddle sores. It was an epic journey to make on a moped. What a test of reliability for the little NSU Quickly, they never missed a beat.

That same summer, Tom and I went by boat from Ardrossan in Scotland, to the famed Isle of Man for the TT races, again astride our faithful NSU Quickly's. This would be the first of many trips to the Island in my future.... more to follow on this subject.

I rode my NSU Quickly to Germany and later to the Isle of Man for the first time in 1955.

I was dabbling in scrambles (moto-cross) and Road Racing now, all on borrowed bikes, and I was active in the Glasgow Mercury Motor Cycle Club, which met on Thursday nights.

After the meeting, a few of us would adjourn to a little café close by, called Lazzarini's. This is where I met Jean, my wife to be. She was gorgeous, and I fell for her right away!

The guys, Alex McGuffie, Duncan Matheson and Eddie Quate, were teasing me all the time, saying that I didn't have it in me to ask Jean to an upcoming Mercury Club dinner/dance. I believed them, and it took me a few weeks to pluck up the courage to ask her. I am happy to say that the rest is history!

In the not too distant future, my apprenticeship would be over. I would be 21 and a fully fledged journeyman at last. But, I would also be going into the British Army for two years National Service, just when I had fallen in love, and starting to think seriously about marriage, and fulfilling the dream I had always nursed, to have my own family at last!

It was now 1957, and I would take one final trip with my three friends, before I had to report for Army service in November. This would be a road trip by car to the Adriatic coast of Italy, to the resort town of Riccione.

Jean and I became engaged shortly after I returned from Italy. We threw a party in conjunction with my 21st birthday. Quite coincidentally, the party took place on Saturday the 21st of September.

Time passed so rapidly, and it was soon November, and I was on my way to the Royal Electrical and Mechanical Engineers basic training camp at Honiton in Devon.

Six weeks later I was heading back to Scotland, fit as a fiddle, and happy in the knowledge that I was to be stationed in Liverpool, a mere 180 miles from Glasgow. I would be able to hitch-hike home on weekends!

Jean, me and my Mother-in-Law Elsie at the Wedding.

"In 1958, half way through my military service, Jean and I decided to get married, and we did so on September 20th 1958........."

In 1958, half way through my military service, Jean and I decided to get married, and we did so on September 20th 1958. I was blissfully happy. We had no money, and left the reception on our one day honeymoon, on a short ride to a reltives

The groom and bride with my dad, the Reverend Isobel Shedden and Gran Ferguson. The Reverend Shedden was the first female minister in Scotland.

house on the other side of Glasgow, in the pouring rain aboard a borrowed motorbike.

It was in fact the very first time that Jean and I had shared a bed. It was a truly special and memorable experience, and only served to convince me even more, that we would someday have a wonderful family of our own.

My two years in Liverpool could have been more exciting, if only I was into rock and roll!

In the 50's, Liverpool was the British rock revolution headquarters, with the likes of the Beatles, Gerry and the Pacemakers, The Searchers, Freddie and the Dreamers, and although Eric Burden and The Animals were from Newcastle, they regularly played on Merseyside.

I must confess that it didn't do much for me, but everyone else was raving about the music, and were off to the Cavern in downtown Liverpool, every weekend they were free from Army duties.

Every chance I got to take off, I would pack my little hold-all, which had "GLASGOW" painted on the side in luminous paint. Then I'd take a bus up to Ormskirk, where north bound traffic merged in those days, and I would begin to hitch-hike my way home to Glasgow.

There were some weird journeys, but in general it was fun, and I would usually be snuggled up to Jean by around midnight.

One summer time hitch-hike I will never forget, I was at my usual spot near Ormskik. I hadn't been waiting very long, when a light blue sports car pulled up. The top was down, and I could tell that the guy was wearing a USAF uniform. He was smiling, and he told me to hop in. He was indeed going to Glasgow in search of his Scottish relatives.

We shook hands, and he explained that he was stationed in Germany and had taken a leave to visit Scotland because he was of Scottish heritage, and hoped he would trace his kinfolk.

He was a Captain, and the car was one I had only seen in magazines, a Chevrolet Corvette Stingray, which he was driving pretty fast. At this rate we would be in Glasgow in no time.

We made a couple of stops on the way. One was near Lockerbie, where he had heard there was a cave. This was the very cave where Robert the Bruce, on the run from the English, watched a spider swinging back and forth, trying desperately, to get across to the other side of the cave. It never gave up, and did make it across eventually. *(According to other historians, it was in hiding on the island of Rachrin, off the Irish coast, that Robert the Bruce was inspired by the spider!)*....I'd like to think that we were in the true place of the historical event!

Legend is that Bruce was so inspired by this spider, that he came out of hiding, and raised another army, to finally defeat the English at the Battle of Bannockburn in 1314. Of course I was aware of the story, but I never knew where the cave was.

"It is unlikely that I would ever have experienced this except for my ride with the Captain in the Stingray!"

It is unlikely that I would ever have experienced this, except for my ride with the Captain in the Stingray!

Jean had a job in Partick, and she would buy me a one way ticket back to Liverpool on the Sunday night train to Lime Street. I would grab a bus in Liverpool and always made it back for muster parade.

12 Command Workshop REME, located in the suburbs of Liverpool, in West Derby, was a big operation. The civilian workforce was around 2.000, the Army a mere 600. It was tough to live with the fact, that the civilians were earning Union scale, whilst the Army guys were making peanuts for the same skills.

In January of 1959, my last year in the service, Jean told me she was pregnant with our first child. I decided that she should join me in Liverpool for a while, and I got permission to live off camp.

Jean returned to Scotland before the arrival of our baby boy on August 29th 1959. His name was David Graham Scott. We were truly on our way to making our own family together, and we still had little or no money!

When I returned to civilian life, I was a changed man. I went back in to my old job, but it was not going to satisfy me anymore. I had learned a very interesting fact during my two years in the service.

REME was a technical regiment, and all my fellow soldier colleagues were graded the same as me, Craftsmen!

I discovered that most of them had long ago ceased working in factories. Even before they were called up for National Service, they had a range of job descriptions, like Technical Sales rep, or Service rep, or even Service Engineer, all of which included a company car or van, and an expense account!

So as soon as I got back in the swing of things, I began browsing through the newspaper ads. There they were…Wanted, Technical rep etc. etc, and I began to write. Why not I thought to myself. I am at the same skill level, and I know that I can do this type of job?

It took me roughly two years of interviews. Almost all of the companies were in England, and seeking a rep for the Scottish territory. I went back and forth on interviews for a long time, until I was called by Fisher and Ludlow in Birmingham. I had made it to the short list. This meant I was in the last three for selection. Here we go at last!

I was to meet for a final interview at St. Enoch's Hotel in Glasgow on December 28th 1961 at 7.15pm. This was it!

I was successful this time, and became one of two Service Engineers for all of Scotland. The other candidate was J.Brian Duffy. I had much to thank the British Army for. If I hadn't been enlightened during that period, I can't imagine what would have become of me. I now had my company car (a Morris Minivan actually) and an expense account. I would never return to a factory ever again.

Jan Mary Elspeth Scott came along on September 8th, 1961, just two months before I landed the new job.

I was racing again, but not very seriously, I had bought a 50cc ITOM just before I went into the Army, and I raced it locally when they had a class. I was still active in the Glasgow Mercury Club, and was in fact the social secretary for a year.

I raced locally on a 50cc ITOM..

My third child, Kimberley McIntyre Scott, was born on September 27th 1962, the same year that Scottish ace bike racer, Bob McIntyre was killed at Oulton Park, hence Kim's middle name.

Life was good, and I stayed with Fisher and Ludlow till 1963, when I was talked into joining my colleague J.Brian Duffy and two others, in a venture named Induvend. I lasted less than a year as a director, and was voted off the board by my fellow directors. They did me a favor however, because the Induvend project failed in 1964, I was not liable for any losses incurred, I dodged a big bullet there!

I had bought a 175cc ex-Vic Camp Ducati and had restored it with a special cam from America. It ran well in the 200cc class, common only to Scotland and Ireland at that time. It got me back in the groove however, but I really wanted a Bultaco 196cc.

After the Induvend fiasco, I was hired by The Ditchburn Organization, who were based in Lytham St.Annes near Blackpool.

While I was at the head office for a week of orientation, my wife called me to break the bad news, that our apartment had been destroyed in a fire. No one was hurt, but many treasures were lost, including most of my racing photos. She didn't want me to curtail my orientation, so I carried on.

Jean and the kids had moved into a summer chalet, owned by her Auntie Jean in Drymen, near Glasgow, so we would live in the country for a while until the apartment was restored. It was really very nice to be away from the big city.

It was now 1965. My fourth child, Allan Roderick Scott, had arrived on February 15th, and I had decided that I would enter the Manx Grand Prix on my Ducati. I had a 250cc engine and would use this.

However we would all have to go to the Isle of Man. It was impossible to afford two places at one time. We would take two large tents and camp in the paddock, simple, right?

Young Allan was just 7 months old when we sailed from Ardrossan in Scotland to Douglas, Isle of Man.

I had a truck, but couldn't afford to bring it also, so I had Neil Nicholson deliver us, and all of my equipment to the dockside, and we loaded our gear onto the deck for the journey. My good friend and fellow racer, Bill Donnelly was shipping his van. His wife Ellen, his kids and bike, were driven aboard.

On arrival in Douglas, Jean and the kids waited on board while Bill and I off-loaded our gear and the bike on to the dock.

He then drove his family and gear up to the paddock camping area, a distance of four or five miles, unloaded his stuff, then came back down to the dock for our gang and gear.

We set up camp and finally got the kids fed, and off to sleep by midnight. It was not raining yet, but it was going to come, and it would rain for almost the full two weeks we were there. Unbelievable and pure misery!

View of the paddock camp grounds with the laundry. The bike is not mine. It is a BSA C.15 that I tested.

"After qualifying, almost immediately I missed a gear at Sarah's Cottage on the second lap. It was race over after two weeks of hell."

After qualifying, almost immediately I missed a gear at Sarah's Cottage on the second lap. It was race over after two weeks of hell.

I walked back down the hill to the Glen Helen Hotel, where the spectators plied me with pints of beer in consolation. I was blasted when Bill Donnelly came to collect me and the bike. Jean was not very happy either. She had had a belly full of the Isle of Man.

The next day we broke camp and Jean and the kids set off down the hill to the Sea Terminal. Bill and I reversed the procedure and got all our various stuff on to the boat for the trip back to Ardrossan, where we would be met by Neil Nicholson and my van,

Poor Jean, the kids were all whimpering and soaking wet. We only had enough for one packet of potato crisps for each of them. I was still in my sodden leathers from the previous day. We had no dry, clean nappies for Allan (cloth diapers). To this very day, I still go to the area where we endured this terrible two weeks at the Manx Grand Prix in 1965!

I was soon back to work at Ditchburn, and earning decent money.

Portion of the program cover for the 1965 Manx Grand Prix on the Isle of Man.

The 1965 Manx Grand Prix was my first race on the Isle of Man, but the first of many trips to the beautiful island in the Irish Sea that would span many decades to this fabled race around this 37-mile island course.

My search for a 196 Bultaco ended when a friend, Neil Nicholson (more about him later), called me up and said that Geoff Monty and Dudley Ward in London, were advertising an ex-Tommy Robb 196 Bultaco, in mint condition.....I already had a buyer for the Ducati.

I got on the phone to Geoff Monty and talked about the bike, telling him that he would never get rid of it in the London area. It would be outclassed in the 250cc class, common to English racing, "so let me take it off your hands", Geoff I said!

I more or less made a deal by telephone, and headed south with Neil Nicholson, hopeful that the bike was as described.

It is 450 miles from Glasgow to London, and of course the bike was nothing like the picture he had painted. I was upset, and Geoff Monty could see this, and he took me into the office and calmed me down.

We hammered out a deal and loaded the bike into the minivan. I had not even heard the bike running, I sure hoped this would work out.

My good friend and sponsor, Alex McGuffie, was a painter, so he took the bike apart, and brought it back to life visually. It looked great. I rebuilt the engine with some tips from other Bultaco owners. We were ready to go. I believe I had the only 196 Bultaco in all of Scotland!

In no time I was right at the front in the 200cc class, winning at Beveridge Park in Kircaldy, Gask, Ingliston and placing in the top five at other tracks.

I had sold my Ducati to Alex George, who was just starting to race, and he wasn't doing too well on the bike. He actually accused me of taking the American cam out, before he bought the bike. I said that was ridiculous, and told him that it was his fault that he was not doing well. I said that he maybe wasn't cut out for racing. However, he would do very well in later life. After I had left for California, he won a TT race for Honda UK in the Isle of Man.

My season had been much more to my liking, and I was looking forward to 1966, and a full year on the Bultaco. I would be traveling with another Bultaco rider, David Catterson, although his was a 125. We would not really race against each other, but I pitted for him and he for me. We would also do a few Irish road races together the next year. Sadly David was killed shortly after I had gone to California at a practice day held at East Fortune racetrack.

"I had also ended the 1965 season as the Scottish Motor Racing Club 200cc Champion and received my trophy from then racing car great *Jim Clark* at the awards banquet in Edinburgh."

Jimmy Clark

I had also ended the 1965 season as the Scottish Motor Racing Club 200cc Champion and received my trophy from then car racing great *Jim Clark* at the awards banquet in Edinburgh.

Early in 1966 Neil Nicholson came to me with a problem. He had been writing as a pen pal to a racer named Bill Boyd in San Francisco for a couple of years, claiming to be a Scottish motorcycle racer. The guy had decided to come for a season of racing in Scotland, at Neil's original invitation, of course.

His plan was to ride at the TT in the Isle of Man in June, and would like to use the Scottish races to get dialed in for the TT. He planned to travel with his fellow pen pal racer Neil, and, he had already shipped his bikes to Prestwick, Scotland, to be collected by Neil Nicholson.

I couldn't believe my ears. How could he have misled this American guy? He confessed right away, that he had literally used my identity for himself, and had written as if he was me!

Neil could play the part for sure. He was never without a motorcycle paper and knew everything about racing history, but he had never raced a bike in his life. He was in big trouble for sure. Who was going to bail him out?

Neil got the notice that the cargo had arrived at Prestwick, and we went down and picked it up. Two large crates, containing three motorcycles and parts.

When we got back to my garage, I could not resist a quick peek inside, so I carefully opened the boxes with a crowbar. It was like we had entered Alladin's Treasure Cave of racing. Inside the first crate was a beautiful Yamaha TD1B, painted polychromatic blue, with Al Fergoda Yamaha, San Francisco on the fairing.

The crate was filled to the top with boxes of spark plugs, cans of oil called Blendzall, never heard of it!

The other crate contained two little Yamaha 100cc twins, street legal with lights and California License plates. We had never seen this model in the UK. Pretty nice set up for this guy and his wife. When they arrived, I hoped I would get to ride one of these 100 twins later. In fact, I later on got a late entry to race one in the Skerries 100 in Ireland, and finished 8th in the handicap, with lights and silencers still in place. What a blast!

I had no alternative but to spill the beans about Neil and his fantasy racing career, and I would do it without delay....well I actually waited until we were sitting down to dinner.

Neil was dying a thousand deaths by now. Bill Boyd and his wife Leslie arrived. My main mission was to quickly assure him that he would not suffer because of Neil, and that all his planning and concerns would now be taken on by me, the actual racer who's identity was stolen by Neil.

"........Bill Boyd would play a major part in my future career, that's another story coming up shortly!"

Bill was killing himself laughing. What a story. He had been writing to Neil for two years. So he actually knew all about ME, not Neil. We were actually old friends, although we had just met. Bill Boyd would play a major part in my future career, that's another story coming up shortly!

I had to find out what he wanted to do, now that he was in the UK. How much was their budget, and how long did he plan to stay here.

He looked at Leslie knowingly. She nodded, and he sheepishly said that they had planned to spend 40 pounds a day between them, until after the TT in June. Would that be enough?...wow!!

If they ran out of money, they could get more from sponsor Al Fergoda, who was coming over for the TT.

I was earning 20 pounds A WEEK, and raising a family on that much!....*or should I now say that little?*

He was an elevator mechanic for Otis Elevator, and Leslie was a Draughtsman, oops! A Draughts person, now in these P.C. times. They both made oodles of money compared to us in the UK.

He wanted to buy a van naturally, and we found one at the auto auction. He loaded up and took off to see a bit of Scotland. I would start to line up local races for him.

Leslie and Bill on their Yamaha 100cc Twins in the pits.

Boyd always ran #69, like Nicky Hayden does today.

We went to the first Scottish race together. I believe it was Crimond, a small airfield circuit.

I watched him getting ready for the first practice session. He warmed the bike up, and then threw away the spark plugs, after fitting the cold race plugs! He was drawing a crowd in his red leathers and bright blue Yamaha anyway, but this caused a near riot, and guys were scrambling for the plugs he discarded.

I told him to stop doing this. We were using the same old plugs, and sandblasting them after every race. I had about 4, and they were over a year old, so he began to hand his used plugs to me from now on.

He also noticed that my bike was smoking, and his was not!

What is your petrol/oil ratio he asked, I said 16 to one. He was laughing like crazy. No wonder you are smoking. I mix mine at 40 to one. And I said that I didn't believe him.

He said to me, empty your tank, and I will mix you some of my oil at 40 to one. I said...No Way Bill, I can't afford to blow up my engine, I will stay with the Castrol R.

Dave, I will buy you a new engine if it blows, using my oil/petrol mixture, and I agreed.

"…….My bike sounded totally different now, and when I took it out in practice, it was absolutely flying."

This was the gold colored can called Blendzall, a synthetic oil from California. My bike sounded totally different now, and when I took it out in practice, it was absolutely flying.

I was a close second in the 200cc race, and the word was out about the oil Everyone wanted to buy the stuff. Too bad guys. I now had the edge for the remainder of the time Bill was in Scotland.

At Crimond, the first race on my Bultaco with "Blendzall", exiting the first turn in second.

He only raced two or three events in Scotland, and I went over to Ireland with him a couple of times. He was enchanted by the true road circuits over there and he said he was going to stay in Ireland for a while.

He had befriended the Yamaha Distributor in Dublin, Southern Ireland, called DANFAY Yamaha. The owners were Danny Feeney and Pheillum McHenry. They too liked Bill Boyd, and began to sponsor him. Bill was in paradise over in Ireland.

We didn't see much more of each other, but every time we did, he was still urging me to come to California, and I began to give it some serious thought. I was doing alright here in Scotland, or so I thought. But it did sound very tempting.

He had been telling his California sponsor, Al Fergoda about me. Al had said he would assist me in anyway he could, with securing a visa, and most attractive of all, he would give me a try out on his team, which I knew was a factory supported operation. He was currently running Englishman Ron Grant and Art Baumann, number one and two in California, on 250cc TD1C Yamaha's, which were not yet in Europe, he also ran a kitted Yamaha 100c twin.

I talked with Jean about all of this, but she was not keen on the idea. I eventually persuaded her to at least let me get the papers from the US Embassy in London. We could fill them in, and I would also see if Al Fergoda was a man of his word. What harm could that possibly do?

"I didn't spend too much time thinking about California....."

I didn't spend too much time thinking about California. Boyd was racing in Ireland, and would be gone after the Isle of Man TT, so nobody was prodding me about leaving the country at this time. I had taken a lucrative new job, servicing slot machines in Casino's and Pubs. The company had an Edinburgh branch, but were really a London based business.

One morning in early July I picked up the Daily Record, Scotland's biggest daily newspaper, and when I got to the classified ads, I almost fainted......a big ad read as follows, "Wanted, skilled toolmakers and machinists for San Francisco area, interviews are being held in the Glassford Hotel etc. etc."

Could this possibly be for real, should I dare to apply? Would I still be able to cut it in an interview, and could I handle the technical test that would follow? Could I possibly do it after being away from the tools for such a long time??

I went to the Glassford Hotel on the morning of the preliminary interviews. The place was packed with candidates. This was not going to be easy, but I pressed on, and eventually spoke with a lady named Doris Law-Bagley. She was the agent in charge of the interview. She was quite charming, and briefly explained that she represented a San Francisco machine shop in dire need of skilled workers.

I told her that I was already in the process of seeking a visa to go to California with my young family. She said that she would make all the visa applications for successful applicants, but she did agree that my existing visa application with the US Embassy could be a plus in my favor.

She would call me back if I was on the short list, hopefully in a day or two, once she had ploughed through this massive crowd.

Doris did call me back and wanted me to return for a technical ability test. It was conducted by an Engineer, whose name I can't remember, but I passed the test, much to my surprise!

Two other guys had made it to the final acceptance stage, Jimmy Gold and Eric Gould. I didn't know either of them, but found them to be nice fellows.

Our deal was as follows. When we received word from the US Embassy to come to London for the physical exam, (this was required back in 1967), and had passed the physical, we would be able to go to the Bank of America branch nearest the Embassy where we would draw $500 for expenses. This had to be paid back within 12 months.

You would also at this time go to the PanAm office, set a travel date, and pick up your pre-arranged paid one way ticket to San Francisco, via New York.

We got the call from the Embassy on the 16th of July, and made an appointment for Thursday July 27th for the physicals and visa issue.

The drive to London in my company car, totally illegal of course, was really hard on Jean and the kids. Then to be subjected to the tests, it was almost too much to take, and Jean was not very keen in the first place.

After we got finished, and had our paper work in hand, I left Jean and the exhausted kids in the park near the Embassy. Then I went off to get my PanAm ticket sorted, and I then collected the $500 cash advance from Bank of America.

It was Thursday afternoon. I would be leaving

Prestwick, Scotland, for New York on Sunday. What's the point of hanging about once you are clear to go?

But first I had to get the kids back home to Glasgow. It was going to be a long night, because when about half way home, near Manchester, the car went on to 3 cylinders, and suddenly became incapable of more than 40 miles per hour. I figured that I had broken a push rod. I would be very lucky to nurse this sick car for another two hundred miles before it would simply blow up!

The kids were becoming nauseous and crying their eyes out. We finally limped into Glasgow at 4am. It had taken us over 11 hours to get home, The car was barely alive at this point.

It was now Friday. I had only two days to wind up my affairs in Scotland. I got on the phone and sold my tools and bike. I did not want anyone to know that I was leaving, and I made all kinds of excuses to the buyers, like I had bought a better bike and the like.

I did get together with the two other guys, on the Saturday before I left, Jimmy Gold and Eric Gould, at a house in Clydebank, I think it was?

After a few drinks, I told them both, that I was not going to go to the job in San Francisco. I had other plans. Just tell the guy that I will repay the $500 as agreed.

I asked my brother-in-law, John Spence, to drive the ailing company car back to Edinburgh and park it at the company, then put the keys through the mail box, and come back to Glasgow by train.

On Sunday morning At Prestwick, the families had gathered to see me off. Most of them on Jean's side were glad to see me gone, others were convinced that I was abandoning my wife and kids. Even Jean may have thought these thoughts. I couldn't blame her for that.

My old man whispered in my ear…."Don't worry about your kids, they will be taken care of, just get on with your new life, who knows, you might be in the movies one day." How right he was, two years later in 1969, I would be in a Paramount movie with Robert Redford called "Little Fauss and Big Halsey".

When I boarded the flight, I had exactly $16 to my name. I had declared 9 pounds sterling. Back in 1967 you had to declare how much you were taking out of the UK. I had given Jean all the money I had, and said that I had no idea when I would send some more. She gave me that knowing look. She had been through a lot with me. This time my new adventure was pretty sizeable, in fact it was the biggest of my life!

"My nine pounds converted to $16 at the money exchange. I sure hope I have enough for a couple of drinks and a phone call......"

My nine pounds converted to $16 at the money exchange. I sure hope I have enough for a couple of drinks and a phone call. What did a phone call cost I wondered?

I had called Bill Boyd from Scotland and told him that I was really coming over, giving him the time and the flight number. He said don't worry buddy, I will meet you at San Francisco. Call me from the airport.

The Captain told us that we would be circling above Kennedy for quite some time. This was typical of Sunday flight density at New York, he said.

Coming through Customs and Immigration for the first time was a memorable, and bitter experience. Rude, arrogant New Yorkers searched my small amount of luggage, pulling out my helmet and leathers and calling all their buddies over to see me explain what they were supposed to be.

If this was typical of America, I was doubtful that I would stay very long over here. San Franciscans dispelled that thought completely when I got there. They were the total opposite, and I was instantly comfortable. I was quite sure that I could make this my new home.

I also shuddered, when I thought about how harrowing it would be for Jean and the four kids, being processed through New York by a bunch of jerks, when they come to join me. Sadly I did not have a clue when that might be!

"I was here. *It was America.* I wondered if it was going to turn out well, or would I be going back to Glasgow with my tail between my legs?"

WELCOME to the United States of America

The Davie Scott Story
California

I was in the air again, on the second leg of my flight, mercifully on my way to San Francisco at last.

My experience with the Immigration and Customs guys in NYC had left me with a bad taste in my mouth. I will never forget how they mocked me, forcing me to put on my black and white ringed European style helmet. Now when I reflect, it seems quite funny, but it was nerve wracking at the time. If I had lost my cool, I could easily have been rejected for entry into the US, right there and then!

My thoughts were also beginning to focus on Bill Boyd. His phone number was the only initial contact I had. Would he be home when I rang, would he actually keep his word and pick me up?

Since his return to San Francisco in 1966, he had survived a nasty accident on the infamous Sunday Morning ride, which runs every Sunday from Stinson Beach to Inverness on Highway-1 in Marin County, and he had lost his left leg!

Embroidered shoulder patch - Sunday Morning Ride.

He had told me of course, and also that he was back on two wheels again, having designed and installed, a street bike with an ingenious hand gear shift. He also was back on the Sunday Morning ride. I couldn't believe it!

I wasn't really sure what to expect when we met again, so immediately on arrival I made the phone call. He was home, and positively delighted that I was at the airport.

Boyd was bound to be different, and I thought I was pretty well prepared for almost anything, however, I was never quite ready for the new Bill Boyd when he arrived with his retinue of maidens!

It was July 1967, the Summer of Love was in full swing in San Francisco, and I was well aware that something unusual was happening over here. But I had no idea I would be swept into the very core of this movement.

Boyd was dressed in a flowing purple velvet robe and wearing a really tall hat. He was carrying what appeared to be an American Indian prayer stick, and his "hand maidens" were fussing over him like he was God.

He was grinning form ear to ear as he introduced me to his now singing entourage. What the hell has happened to change the straight arrow, dedicated, no sex before races, modest professional racer I used to know. The answer was simple, the drug and Hippy culture was raging here in San Francisco, and he had assumed a completely new lifestyle!

We all piled into his old station wagon, which was decorated with hand painted flowers and peace signs. There were lots of similar vehicles all over California. People were flocking to San Francisco from all over the country, come to think of it, from all over the World in fact.

Scott McKenzie was topping the pop music charts with his rendition of "If you come to San Francisco, be sure to wear a flower in your hair."

What a contrast to my initial experience of America, which I was served up in New York by that group of officials!

"Boyd lived right in the heart of it all, Frederick Street in the Haight-Ashbury district, in what could only be described as a commune, housing the strangest cross section of humanity imaginable."

Boyd lived right in the heart of it all, Frederick Street in the Haight-Ashbury district, in what could only be described as a commune, housing the strangest cross section of humanity imaginable.

There had to be at least fifty residents, coming and going at all hours. People were knocking on the door all the time, buying weed, and probably other things. I was given a space on the floor of a room, and a sleeping bag. This would be my new California home. I went to sleep that night deep in thought, what the hell lies ahead in the days to come?

In the morning I opened one eye, and could hardly believe what I was seeing, a uniformed San Francisco policeman, a Sergeant in fact, was just strapping on his belt and gun. I almost died of shock, and assumed that we had all been busted while I slept!

He noticed that I was awake, and he bent down, reaching out his hand to introduce himself. "Welcome to San Francisco, my name is Dick Burgess, but everybody calls me Sergeant Sunshine!"

This was going to be one of my room mates!!!

He explained briefly that he was currently estranged, from his wife and kids, and had found this fabulous new way to live. He had simply dropped out, well not quite totally, he was still a cop, but planned to quit that as well.

He said he had to go to work, but he would take me out tonight for a look at the city. He was a really friendly guy, probably because he was high all the time!

Boyd was trying like crazy to get me to try Marijuana, LSD, Hashish, Cocaine and a wide selection of other drugs. I told him that there was no chance that I would try any of this stuff, my poison was beer and wine!

This was my second day in San Francisco and Boyd was taking me to meet Al Fergoda at the Yamaha dealership on Market Street. I was looking forward to this.

Fresh in from Scotland, I was in stark contrast to Boyd and his group, short hair, conventional dress. I think Boyd's friends thought I was a Narcotics agent.

Al Fergoda seemed relieved about my appearance. He knew I was coming over, and probably thought I would be another long hair Hippy too!

He told me that he had sent in the visa forms a while back, and I thanked him. I would explain later how I got to San Francisco so quickly.

He told me almost at once that there was a race at Cotati this coming Sunday, and he would like me to ride his 250, and possibly the 100. I was ecstatic to say the least. The pace of my new life was astonishing, but very much to my liking.

He walked me to the race shop. There sat two Yamaha TD1C's, both fitted with Fontana brakes.

Betty and Al Fergoda at their Golden Wedding Anniversary with their son George and daughter Joy.

I knew that only TD1B models were available in the U.K. This was the latest 250, with the clutch on the gearbox, not on the crankshaft….wow!

The little 100 twin was a jewel, and the personal project of the team mechanic Mario Campetti, who was also an immigrant like me. Mario arrived from Italy just a few years ago and was a really fine technician with a gigantic ego. My nickname for him was Mussolini.

But he was a kind man at heart, and we got along quite well, Al was asking me what I planned to do, and I told him I simply hadn't figured it out yet. He suggested I come to work at the dealership. I could keep the place tidy, sweep the floors, help in general.

I was a little put out by this idea. After all I was a skilled tool maker, and this was a bit beneath me. He laughed and said that he would pay me $100 a week to do this work, a rapid mental calculation revealed to me that this was around 60 British pounds!

I had been a top earner, making 30 pounds a week in Scotland, and raising a family, and racing!

"……..However, it only lasted a week or so before I was on the Sales floor, and selling lots of Yamahas. What a meteoric start to my new California life."

Right away I promised Al that he would get the best clean up man he had ever hired, and I was indeed. However, it only lasted a week or so before I was on the Sales floor, and selling lots of Yamahas. What a meteoric start to my new California life.

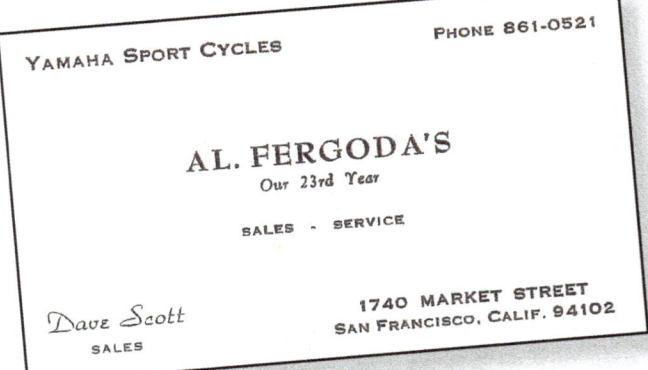

Boyd had mentioned that we were all going to go to a drive-in movie tonight. I had heard of drive-ins, but had never been to one There was nothing like this in Scotland.

We all piled into the old station wagon and headed off to the Geneva drive-in, located in Daly City. We stopped just before the entrance, and a few of the guys got in the back, and were covered up by blankets. Only two people payed, the rest got in for free!

I had a six pack of beer, and the others were all smoking dope. A short time after the feature film began, a message flashed up on the big screen… "Bill Boyd please come to the manager's office, this is urgent".

One of Al Fergoda's office employees, named Tom McIlhatten, who was a close friend of Boyd's, had driven past the apartment on Frederick Street, and the place was swarming with law enforcement. He thought they were probably Narcotics men, who were raiding the place!

My heart sank when I heard this. All of my belongings, in particular my passport and visa, were in a cupboard at the apartment. I was probably about to be deported after no more than two days in the country. It was absolutely unbelievable!

We had a brief discussion about what to do. Tom said that I should not risk going back to Boyd's place. I could come home to his parent's house in the Sunset district and he would introduce me while he explained the situation.

They very kindly allowed me to stay there overnight, and in the morning, Tom took me on a drive past the house on Frederick Street. It appeared that everything was back to normal, no police in sight. As I went nervously up the stairs, I plucked up the courage to knock on the door.

Boyd opened the door, with that big infectious grin on his face again. The police were actually looking for some dangerous criminal, and had been systematically raiding the whole area. It was not about drugs.

I went to the cupboard and retrieved my brief case. Everything was intact. Did the cops ever search my belongings? Did they notice that I had just arrived in the USA? Would they tell Immigration I was living in a drug commune? That thought haunted me for a very long time!

When I finally got to work, Al had already heard the story and warned me to be cautious with Bill Boyd, who he now considered a totally lost cause, and a mere shadow of the man he used to be!

How could I have so innocently walked into a potential visa violation, let alone possible jail time, and instant deportation back to Scotland? Was I ever living a charmed life or not?

I was having a great time, selling new and used bikes. The customers came in all shapes and sizes, Hippy, Gay and Lesbian, some who had never ridden before, which meant I had to load their new bike onto the truck and teach them to ride, usually in the parking lot of nearby Kezar Stadium. Great fun all around.

At the end of day four of my stay in San Francisco, Al was getting ready to lock up the dealership, when he handed me $5 and sent me to the local drug/liqour store. "Bring back a pint of Dewar's White Label", he said. This became a ritual, each evening at the close of business, Al and I would relax and polish off the pint of Dewars. I never really drank whisky in Scotland, but I was learning fast!

"Sergeant Sunshine, *Dick Burgess*, was true to his word, and took me on a tour of the city night life........"

Sergeant Sunshine, Dick Burgess, was true to his word, and took me on a tour of the city night life (in plain clothes). He also treated me to two pairs of blue jeans from Sears. I had never owned denims before, but it was the normal, everyday garb amongst my new friends.

Dick also took me to a town in the East Bay called Walnut Creek. It seemed like paradise to me, warm and sunny, and his wife and kids lived in this beautiful house, complete with a swimming pool.

He was visiting his family home to pay his child support, and play with his kids for a while. But it was obvious that there was hostility between him and his wife, so we were soon on the road back to San Francisco. However, I would always remember Walnut Creek, and I promised myself that I would live there someday, and we did!

Back at work the next day, the race shop was busy getting ready for Sunday's race, I was to meet Ron Grant for the first time this day. He was of course known to me, via the Motorcycle magazines, and I was well aware that he was originally from London.

He was one of the most self confident men I have ever met, a tall guy, who seemed to constantly bounce around, always cracking jokes, which everyone seemed to laugh along with. I had him pegged for a typical Cockney barrow boy, a hustler type of guy.

"........Scott, I never see you race yet, but I tell you one thing, you cannot beat Ron"....."Nobody can beat Ron."

My first race in America!....The Al Fergoda 250cc Yamaha at Cotati. Push-starting at far left below at the Vaca Valley Raceway AFM style.... and it's always nice to win one's first race!

Mario, the race mechanic loved Ron Grant, and told me straight…"Scott, I never see you race yet, but I tell you one thing, you cannot beat Ron"……"Nobody can beat Ron."

I thought it was a joke Italian style, but he was dead serious, and told me that I would see what he meant on Sunday at Cotati. I could hardly wait!

The bike I was to ride was usually ridden by Art Baumann, who I had just heard was fired by Al for stupidly blowing up the race truck when he failed to add engine oil. Art had argued with Al about it, a fatal mistake.

My 250 was already showing a fresh new number 15s on the fairing, my very own new American Federation of Motorcyclists National number (issued right away because I had an FIM license from Geneva). I was raring to go!

One thing that was troubling me was the left side gear shift lever. To counter my concern, I was riding street bikes every day with this shift set up, and it did not seem too awkward to handle. Under race conditions however, it might be very different. Mario flatly refused to switch it over for me. I would have to live with it.

Cotati was a small town located off highway 101, about 50 miles north of San Francisco. The circuit was laid out on an old airfield, not very complex in nature, and quite similar to airfield circuits in Scotland and England. I learned it quite quickly and felt right at home here. The weather was extremely hot, around 95 degrees.

I thought that I might have a problem with this, in my all black leathers, and being fresh in from the much colder Scottish climate. But I was completely wrong, I loved the heat, and would never ever suffer in this extremely contrasting weather.

Ron Grant and I took off and disappeared in the race. Nothing could match the Fergoda factory backed Yamahas. It was incredible for me. I had spent most of my racing life trying desperately to keep up with far superior bikes, ridden by what I considered less talented riders, only to have them blow past me on the straightaways.

Now I was aboard one of the best bikes in the whole country, and I was exuberant. All I had to do was be calm, get to know this fantastic machine, and try to catch and beat Ron Grant, a very tall order perhaps!

Grant was playing with me, staying slightly ahead, and turning round to wave to me, lap after lap, it was a unique experience for me. I had never played games like this when ever I went racing. I treated it very seriously. This was crazy riding!

He was currently the best road racer in California, and I already knew that I would have to beat him, perhaps not today, but sometime in the future. With this bike I felt that anything was possible, so I was happy to let Grant fool around. I was solid in second place.

I had always believed that even the best riders in the world could rarely overcome a second rate bike. I was now learning in fact, that I was a pretty good rider after all, on this kind of bike, racing was a pleasure.

Two laps from the end of the race I saw a puff of smoke coming from Grant's bike. He had probably over revved the engine during his showboating antics. His race was over, and I took the checkered flag. My first ever race in California was a victory. It doesn't get any better than that?

Al Fergoda was standing at the finishing line, holding out a big blackboard, upon which was pictured a Martini glass with a cherry on a stick, and a big Dollar sign, as I took the flag, I could see that he was happy!

On the 100cc Yamaha Twin.

Glancing over at #1 Ron Grant.

AFM races ran in the rain. I was completely at home in the wet.

#58 Jody Nicholas was the rider I replaced in the movie.

"My win on Sunday cemented my relationship with Al, and Yamaha International in Los Angeles."

My win on Sunday cemented my relationship with Al, and Yamaha International in Los Angeles.

When I showed up for work on Monday, everyone was congratulating me, even Mario seemed pleased. The boss was looking for me too.

Al told me to sit down for a minute. He wanted to talk to me about my family in Scotland. How many kids I had. He already knew I was married of course, and wondered what I had planned for Jean and the kids.

I told him that I was simply going to have to save money and eventually bring them over. He seemed relieved, but looked me in the eye, and asked me straight, "are you dumping that family of yours"?

Not a chance I told him, and showed him pictures of my two girls and two boys, and their beautiful mother. I told him I had no idea how long it was going to take, but I would get them here someday, by hook or by crook!

He sent me back to work. There were people in the showroom who had been at the Cotati races and were looking to buy bikes. I obliged, and sold two that day, This was a perfect example of racing producing retail sales. Race on Sunday, buy on Monday. I had just proved it happens.

After lunch, Al called me back into the office again. He wanted more information. What city in Scotland, ages of our children, their names, how long did I think Jean would need to get it together and fly out of Scotland?....and then he sent me back to the showroom once more!

It was Monday August 7th. I had completed my first week in San Francisco. At the end of the work day I had the customary few drinks with Al. He told me that he really liked me and wanted to help me bring my family over. I said that would be terrific, but I didn't get any more out of Al.

The next day he told me he had spoken to PanAm and had found out that Prestwick was the nearest transatlantic departure point for Glasgow. If my wife and kids had tickets to SFO from there, could they get to Prestwick. I said I was sure that the rest of our combined families would get them to Prestwick.

This conversation was getting crazy. I said, what is the point Al, I don't have the means to do anything like this. At that point he pulled out his wallet and let a considerable selection of credit cards tumble onto his desk. You might not, but I sure as heck have, he said!

Where would you live he asked? I said that I hadn't a clue. But one of the mechanics, Bob Breslin, had noticed a house on his street in Daly City was available for rent, and he had mentioned it to me. Al told Bob to find out the details after work tonight. How big it was, how much rent, and Bob said he would.

For the next week, Al was calling me in to ask me more questions, and I was still saying to him that this was an exercise in futility. Why are we getting so intense, for I considered the whole thing to be completely out of my reach?

The following Monday, August 14, I was back in his office. This time he showed me a flight departure itinerary for Jean and the four kids. They were booked to leave Prestwick on Friday the 18th, next FRIDAY!

"I was speechless, Jean would never believe this, and would most likely refuse to go along with it!......he said, "call her right now, Scotsman"!

I was speechless, Jean would never believe this, and would most likely refuse to go along with it!......he said, "call her right now, Scotsman"!

He would arrange for the tickets to be delivered by PanAm courier. Was she sure she could get to the airport. If not, let's get a limo he said. I assured him that they would get to Prestwick, and I called her right there and then with the news.

Right away she thought I was drunk!......and didn't believe a single word. I asked her how she could possibly think that I would pull a joke of this seriousness. I told her I would call back the next day, to make sure that their tickets were delivered....seeing is believing?

Al was relishing every moment of what had become his personal project, however, I was in a spin, and wondering how it could all get done by Friday!

Al's daughter, Joy, took me to see the vacant apartment in Daly City. It was a really nice quiet neighborhood, close to a school also. The place was perfect, far, far better than my Glasgow apartment. The rent seemed affordable too, but they required first and last months rent, and a security deposit, and of course, I had no money!

Joy asked me if I was absolutely sure that this place would suit my family. I said yes, but I don't have the money to lock in the rental agreement. She promptly pulled out a Fergoda Yamaha company check and gave the landlord the necessary amount. I signed the papers. I now had an apartment for sure, BUT no furniture, in fact no nothing!

Joy let me hang back for a while, and I looked the empty apartment over. It sure was a nice place, I thought to myself. I will borrow a sleeping bag and stay here tomorrow night. Just four days left to furnish the apartment. It was impossible I felt, it was going to take a miracle for sure, but at least I would have Jean and the kids here. We would make it work somehow. This was turning into a fairy tale!

At work on Tuesday August 15, Al congratulated me on finding a suitable apartment, and I thanked him for putting up the money needed, and for Joy's help. I also assured him that I would pay every penny back to him.

I told him that I had to phone Jean, to see if the tickets were there. He said do it now.

The tickets had been delivered, and Jean was speechless. But she was now a believer. This was no joke, she was heading for San Francisco in 3 days!

I told her to dress the kids neatly, but don't bring lots of baggage. We would start from scratch in California. Simply give all of our Scottish worldly goods, away to friends and family, and start thinking about her new life. I told her I had a wonderful apartment waiting for them. I did not tell her that we had nothing in the apartment, that would have been fatal at this stage.

I told Al that I was going to stay at the apartment tonight. He said that he and his wife Betty were planning to come over and see the place, so I was to be sure that I went directly there after work. I agreed to meet them.

I got there at 6.30p.m., and not much later, Al and Betty arrived. They were not alone. There were several cars and vans with them, and they were starting to unload furniture, carpets, bunk beds, lamps, pictures, in fact everything imaginable that I would require to furnish my apartment. Complete strangers in most cases, were furnishing my new home. One person filled the refrigerator (which we never had in Scotland). Others assembling and making beds, hanging blinds and curtains. I was totally overwhelmed, to this very day, I get emotional when I talk about this incredible act of kindness.

By midnight, it was done, and we were all pretty drunk, I tried to put words together, to express my sincere gratitude and thanks, but Al said.." Listen kid, this is America, if people kinda like someone, they will give you anything, but if they don't like you buddy, you get nothing"

"What a start to our new life in California……It would be exactly 19 days since I left Scotland with $16!"

What a start to our new life in California. I had a good job, I won my very first race. My family had a nicely furnished apartment to come to, and would be with me this Friday August 18th. It would be exactly 19 days since I left Scotland with 16 dollars!

There is an expression I use quite frequently these days, when something really unusual or bizarre happens. I say "Only in America". This was truly one of those times in my life, and it was all due to a series of unlikely connections.

The Neil Nicholson fiasco with his make believe letters to Bill Boyd, the San Francisco job opportunity, the once in a life time chance to prove my ability on a real racing motorcycle, and the tremendous generosity of Al Fergoda. I'm getting emotional just writing this account of my unbelievable luck.

I went to SFO with Al in his Cadillac Eldorado (he called it his Jew Jeep). My gang arrived looking completely bewildered and exhausted from the long trip. The kids had thought they were only going for a day trip on an airplane.

So they were in for a shock when they suddenly discovered that they would not be able to visit their Nanny tomorrow as usual. I would do my best to explain it all to them. It sure was nice to see Jean too. I knew she must have been through hell in NYC with the Immigration guys.

But she said they treated her well. It was the ignorant taxi driver, who took them across to the other terminal to transfer for SFO, and made her unload her own bags while she struggled with the kids. She had just the exact amount in dollars left, not enough for a tip!

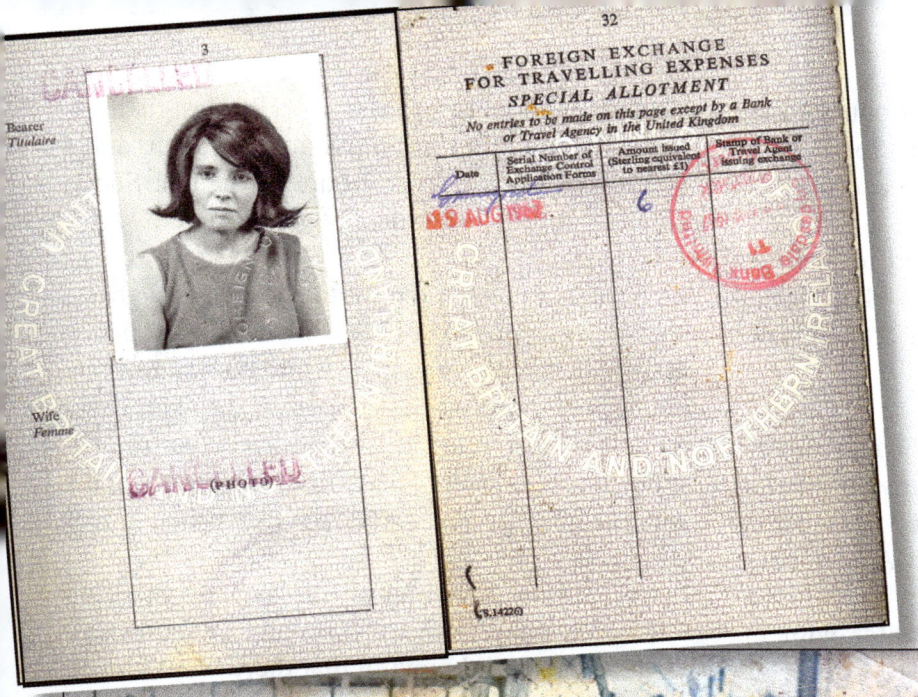

International Raceway. Ontario was not yet in existence, and I was racing in the San Francisco area at Vaca Valley Raceway and Cotati once a month.

Jean was not doing so well. She and the kids were very homesick for quite a long time. Her days were long, until I came home from work. Once in a while, I would take her to the Edinburgh Castle Pub in San Francisco to mingle with Scottish people who congregated there. It was like a tonic to her.

I stayed with the Al Fergoda Yamaha job and racing team till 1969 when he sold the whole race shop and equipment to a guy called Harry Hunt. I also went with the deal.

Before he sold out, I had talked Al into getting one of the new TR2 350cc Yamahas. There were only a few allocated to selected dealers.

Our first outing to San Francisco's Fisherman's Wharf. (L-R) Me, Kim, Allan, Jean, David, Ricky Campetti and Jan. Ricky was the son of Mario, our race mechanic.

When I left Scotland just 19 days ago with $16, I had no idea that Jean was even more broke than me. She had just $12 to her name. I do remember telling her to give everything away to friends and family, and she did!

I spent quite a lot of time on this particular story because it is so rich with the goodness and kindness that I am sure exists in everyone, but rarely is seen or activated. I hope everyone grasps the enormity of my good fortune on arrival in California.

Life was a mad whirl, especially for me. I was racing in Southern California at least once a month, Willow Springs, Riverside and Orange County

I wanted to ride in the Daytona 200 in March 1969. He agreed to send the 250 and the new 350. The Yamaha TR2 was not yet available in Europe.

When the crate, containing the TR2 arrived at the Yamaha store, we couldn't get it open quick enough. It was the most beautiful bike I had ever seen.

It was painted in the Yamaha factory colors, white, with a broad red stripe running down the length of the tank, and the same on the bucket seat, exactly the same as the factory bikes I had seen Bill Ivy and Phil Read riding in Europe, it was gorgeous!

Al came through from his office to check it out against the invoice he was clutching, and he was moaning about the price he paid!

And that's my dealer cost too, how could I have let you talk me into paying this much for a bike? I never did ask how much it actually cost him!

The bike also came with a kick-start lever fitted, and an owner's manual with quotes like…"to attain maximum speed, rider should crouch down behind perspex window".

We tested at the newly constructed Sears Point circuit before loading up for the long drive to Florida. I would be back to this new track in September for the inaugural motorcycle race, an AMA National.

Daytona would be my first encounter with the AMA national riders, such as Cal Rayborn, Gary Nixon, Bart Markel, Gene Romero and a host of other famous U.S. stars. They were primarily dirt track racers, in pursuit of the AMA National Championship. They had to road race too, if they wanted points for the championship. Not all of them enjoyed road racing.

I quickly found out that I had nothing to fear. They were all humans, not gods after all, and I was up amongst them with little difficulty. Rod Gould from England was also there. Both of us fell foul of the scrutineers at technical inspection. My Jim Lee framed TD1C had never been seen before at Daytona. We went through hell to get it approved.

Rod and I both had black leathers, and we were told we would have to wear satin colored vests, or paint white stripes down the arms of our leathers. I went to a drug store and bought tennis shoe whitener, and we painted each other.

The 250 race was on Saturday. I blew an engine late in qualifying, and it was touch and go to fit another motor before I was shoved onto the back row of the grid for the race.

Doug Schwerma had prepared the engines, and they were fast. However, when the guys had fitted the shift lever, they did not know what angle I was used to, so they just stuck it on any spline, hopeful that it was correct, it was not!

Doug Schwerma, incidentally, was considered to have perfected the 5 port cylinder design for two strokes, mainly for Yamaha's. His design mysteriously ended up in production in Japan, and I doubt that he was ever credited for this. Sadly, Doug committed suicide a few years later.

As soon as I pressed the shift lever into 2nd gear, I knew it was going to be nearly impossible to operate like this. I was trying to cope while carving my way through the pack when it started to sprinkle. I was in luck, or so I thought. I would have a terrific advantage now, because I had raced many times in the wet. Imagine my anger when the race was stopped!

It was raining big time on the Sunday morning of race day, and we Europeans and Canadians all went to the track knowing that there would be no racing in the rain.

The fans were throwing chairs from the grandstands after the organizers announced that the race would take place in one week's time. Many of the riders stayed in Daytona or went to the nearby Bahamas. Al wanted me back at the dealership. Yamaha would pay us to come back next week.

We were told to put all the factory supported Yamaha bikes and equipment in a secure garage, and we would jet back to SFO on Monday morning.

Every evening of Daytona Speed Week Roxy Rockwood had a one hour radio show at the Castaways Hotel, during which he introduced celebrities and racers. The Sunday night of the postponement was a wild show with riders taking sides for and against racing in the rain.

When I took the stage, I had had a few whisky's, and I set about verbally lambasting those who had voted against racing. I knew who all the stars were, and I unleashed a torrent of abuse on them. The place went wild. Little brawls and scuffles were happening all over the ballroom. Roxy was loving every minute of it!

Harley Davidson factory rider Bart Markel jumped on the stage beside me. He shouted that I was right. He didn't really know who I was, but he was backing this guy (me) who spoke funny. We both reckoned they were a bunch of chickens, and I personally lost all respect for those so called stars.

I later found out that Cal Rayborn, the Harley star, and favorite to win the 200, was nursing a broken collarbone. This postponement would give him extra time to heal. He did in fact win the race a week later. Harley Davidson had a lot of influence on the AMA in those days. They wanted to make sure their boy would win!

I had qualified on the third row of the grid, right amongst those Harley team riders. I was hoping they would let bygones be bygones when I showed up next week!

It was a little crazy to fly all the way back to Florida, but that was the way Al wanted it. It was a long week to kill time. I thought the weekend would never get here.

When we got back to Daytona and showed up at the Yamaha garage, there was quite a collection of well known riders. Yvon DuHamel, who rode for Canadian Distributor Fred Deeley, Rod Gould, Dick Mann.

My bike had a front wheel balance problem, and Goodyear had spent a lot of time trying to balance it, but couldn't figure it out.

I would find out much later, from Australian Jack Findlay, the future new owner of this bike, that the brake drum casting had been improperly machined at the factory in Japan, and was in fact out of round, in relationship to the axle. No amount of counterweights would ever balance this wheel, and I had simply lived with the front wheel dancing about at high speed on the banked oval. It was scary!

Off the line: #3 Roger Rieman, #111 Don Vesco, #73 Davey Scott and #4 Bart Markel.

On the infield section of Daytona, I did not notice the front wheel bouncing, and I cannot say for certain that it was the cause of my crash entering the banked oval from the infield.

"I was having a teriffic duel with Nationbal Champion Gary Nixon on his factory Triumph......"

I was having a terrific duel with National Champion Gary Nixon on his factory Triumph, I could pull away on the straights, but he would catch me on the brakes and cornering. We were still in sight of the leaders though, and running in 9th and 10th. Gary would eventually finish 9th.

I was running 9th and Gary Nixon 10th. Gary would eventually finish 9th.

It happened so quickly. I was leaned over, and scraping the left expansion chamber. I did this every lap, it was unavoidable.

".......in a flash, I was over the handlebars, headed for the straw bales, not able to get my arms in front of me to cushion my impending impact!"

I believe the suspension compressed a bit further on this particular lap, and my left exhaust chamber made heavy contact this time. It was more severe this time.....in a flash, I was over the handlebars, headed for the straw bales, not able to get my arms in front of me to cushion my impending impact!

My face, chin and teeth hit the asphalt, the bike was barely damaged. I must admit, that just for a millisecond, I reflected on my recent refusal to wear the new full coverage helmets on offer!

I was dazed when the marshals got to me, and I was staring down at the blood, and right in the middle of the pool, there were several teeth in plain view!

They were loading me into the ambulance when Ron Pierce came around in the lead, and promptly fell off, I suspect when he ran over my teeth and blood. The press said Ron's crash was caused by fluid from my Yamaha. I know better than that!

Ron Pierce leading the Daytona 200 shortly before falling in my blood and teeth!

The most severe damage was facial, and I was taken to the infield medical center, where they dressed the other abrasions. My face however, was too serious for them, and they sent me by ambulance to nearby Halifax General Hospital.

Al Fergoda came with me, and I told him to be sure that I was going to be on the flight home with him tomorrow. I assured him that after I get patched up today, I would sign myself out of the hospital. I had no intention of being left here in Daytona.

I also told Al to go back and enjoy the post race party, and have a good time. I looked really gruesome, but I was not quite at deaths door, thank goodness!

The hospital let me call Jean before any surgery was performed. I warned her that I was a ghastly sight, and not to keep the kids up, when I came home on Monday evening.

My facial repair would be performed by a plastic surgeon. He was on a golf course nearby, and showed up in his golf gear. Alas, I don't remember his name, but he made me overcome my mental anxiety immediately, and I surrendered to his procedures.

First came the pictures, for the "before and after" record, and for the San Francisco follow-up specialist.

Then he explained that he was going to snap-off the remaining upper teeth, because they were in the way, and I really would need dental surgery back in San Francisco, wow!

He was talking to me all the time, joking and laughing, telling me how good I was going to look in a couple of weeks. I didn't believe him for one moment.

He next lifted skin, from my right buttock, to graft onto my upper lip and chin, making some corny joke about it. I wanted to laugh, but couldn't manage it. It all took about 4 hours, and I looked even worse in the mirror, but he absolutely insisted, that I would barely see any scars in a couple of weeks.

I called Al, and gave him the news about my surgery, and I also repeated my intention to be on his flight tomorrow.

I spent a good night at Halifax Hospital, but they were very upset with me, when I got dressed early in the morning, and signed myself out.

Al took me back to the hotel to pack and eat breakfast. I had only a small opening to my mouth, so I had a double Scotch and soda, and drank it through a straw. It would be a while before I could eat solids!

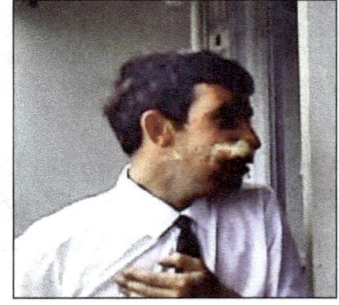

Al Fergoda and I preparing to fly home Monday morning.

It wasn't easy to get accepted by the airlines in my condition, but after three tries, Al got clearance from Delta, and we were off to Dallas on the first leg. The pain was excruciating when we were at altitude. Only a bunch more Scotch and sodas helped me bear the misery. My wounds were also beginning to seep through the dressing, and were dripping onto my collar. Passengers were aghast. When I walked back to the toilet, this was awful for them and me!

I called my brother Jack from Dallas, and asked him to bring a pillow case with him.

Jack and his family had recently moved from Scotland to California, where he continued his trade as a journeyman machinist, moving near to me in Daly City.

When he came to pick me up at SFO, I didn't feel that I could stand all the gasping and gaping that would likely take place on the way to his car!

Jean was unable to make the kids go to bed. They knew I was coming home, and wanted to greet me before bedtime. Those poor kids freaked out when they saw me, even the dog ran away and hid!

At home with my brother Jack with his family with me and my family at Easter, three weeks after my crash.

During this period of recovery we found a nice home across the bay in Walnut Creek and made the move.

The surgeon was right. Within a few weeks I was healed up, toothless mind you, but looking fine, and I was back on the bike racing, none the worse mentally from the crash!

Another fine act of kindness and generosity came about when Dudley Perkins. Sr, a long time friend of Al's, and the current San Francisco Harley Davidson dealer, arranged for me to have major dental surgery performed at a top notch specialists on Sutter Street in the city. They operated on my mouth for four hours, inserting more than fifty stitches. I was back on a liquid diet again, just when I had managed to chew steak with my gums?

Dudley paid for everything. Within a month I had dentures successfully fitted for the first time. It was a fine gesture by Mr. Perkins.

Al's enthusiasm was deflated by my accident however, and decided to sell the whole race shop, lock, stock and barrel. Thankfully, Al made sure that the deal included me.

SIDEBAR

Gary Nixon and I got back together on the Isle of Man in 1993, 24 years after we raced together at Daytona.

Harry Hunt was the new team owner, a pretty nice guy, known in the San Francisco area, as a wealthy motorcycle enthusiast.

He had been in Europe for a number of years, representing the US Government's interests in

International financial affairs, and International banking. He was based in Brussels, Belgium I believe.

While he was in Europe, he befriended well known Australian continental circus rider, Jack Findlay and his lady Nanou Lyonard, and I believe he may have helped sponsor Jack also.

"…….He nearly killed me a few times in the early days of our two year relationship………."

So he was experienced in the ways of racing at world level, but not a very skilled hands-on engineer. He nearly killed me a few times in the early days of our two year relationship when he overlooked safety wiring, the top rings of carburetors, or sprockets, and master link clips, stuff like that!

He was also a personal friend of Daniele Fontana, the Italian brake manufacturer, and he became the US distributor for those great brakes.

Harry upgraded the TD1C's immediately, to the new TD2 Yamaha model. This model was still not available in Europe. I thought the old TD1C was a terrific bike, but this new TD2 was awesome, especially when Harry threw away the stock Yamaha brakes and fitted Fontana's. I would win a lot of races on this 250. Sadly, I could not say that I achieved the same results with the new TR2 350. It was a different bike altogether, and I never truly enjoyed it as much as the 250.

However, Harry's bikes would help me win the American Federation of Motorcyclists Championship in 1970. I would ride with the number one plate in 1971.

When Al sold the team to Harry Hunt, my brother Jack and I bought the little Fergoda Yamaha 100 twin, primarily to get ahold of the one-of-a-kind 6-speed gear cluster, which Al had purchased at the factory, on one of his visits to Hamamatsu, Japan. We hoped it would fit in our project racer, a TA125 Yamaha production racer.

We had married the 125 Yamaha engine to an air-cooled Bultaco TSS125 frame. After a very long search for the used Bultaco frame, we fitted baby Fontana brakes, Ceriani forks, and a host of good parts. Sadly, the gear cluster did not fit!

A fellow ex-racer and recent Scottish emigrant, named Dave Duncan, had been helping on the project, and felt that he might make the gear cluster fit.

He said he would take the two crankcases, and the cluster, to the tool room where he worked, and see what he could do.

My brother Jack and I knew that he was a top notch engineer, and sure enough, after a few weeks, he proved this to us. When he brought the two half crankcases back, the cluster was in, and working perfectly, but it would still be a while before we would race it.

However, we now had the only six speed Yamaha 125 twin in this part of the world, and I can't be certain that it may have been the only six speeder anywhere at that time?

The highly skilled engineer Dave Duncan installed the rare 6-speed cluster after much difficulty.

1969 was going to be an interesting season indeed. I was preparing for another shot at the AMA National stars. They would be coming to Sears Point in September. I had already tested there, and liked the layout of the circuit, I should have an edge at Sears.

A couple of weeks before the event, Roxy Rockwood, who was also the P.R. guy at Yamaha International in L.A., asked me to come down and talk to him, he said he had a deal for me.

Yamaha wanted me to ride Harry Hunt's bikes in a Paramount movie starring Robert Redford. I would be paid well for a week of stunt doubling prior to the big National. I flatly refused!

I was going to Sears Point to try and win. I was a contender with a very good sponsor. It was out of the question, and that was that, or so I thought!

Ten days before the race, Roxy called again, and said that they had signed Jody Nicholas, National number 58, to do the part, but he was a Naval reservist, and had suddenly been called for service, aboard an aircraft carrier somewhere in the Pacific.

So what? I asked him. He said that Jody and I were the same size, and I was the only other AMA Expert rider who would fit into the leathers to be worn in the movie. I knew that Yamaha was in a bind, and agreed to do it, subject to Harry Hunt's o.k.

"I asked Jean who the heck Robert Redford was, and she almost swooned when I told her I would be working with him in this Paramount movie!"

I asked Jean who the heck Robert Redford was, and she almost swooned when I told her I would be working with him in this Paramount movie!

Harry had to have the bikes painted to match the movie script. He was very reluctant to even be involved in this whole thing, but he knew I could use the money, and he went along with it.

The whole week of filming was in 100 degree weather. There was never a single scene that satisfied the director. It was always…do it again, and again, and again!

I was actually double/stunt riding for a guy called Michael J. Pollard, who you may remember was the driver in Bonnie and Clyde.

The director was always looking for near impossible results. Even the official Hollywood stunt rider was turning down certain very difficult tasks.

I rode #58, playing the part of actor Michael J. Pollard's "Little Fauss" in the Paramount picture "Little Fauss and Big Halsey".

Close friend Bill Donnelly

Brother Jack

I made quite a bit of extra money performing some of these. My fellow racers, who were watching, said I was nuts to risk my life for theses Hollywood crazies!

During the week I had become friendly with Redford, and told him that Jean adored him, even though I had never heard of him. He laughed about that.

I knew we were invited to a private Paramount enclosure on race weekend when the movie was hopefully completed, and I asked him if he would be around when my wife arrived with our kids.

He told me to come to his trailer when they arrived, and show him where she and the kids were. I let Jean wander ahead, as I knocked on his trailer.

I pointed her out to him. There he was, stripped to the waist, bandana and cowboy hat parked back on his head, just as he appeared in most of the movie scenes.

He snuck up behind her, and put his arms around her, slowly turning her to face him, and he introduced himself. The look on her face will stay with me forever, what a great guy he was. The movie by the way was called. "Little Fauss and Big Halsey".

I can never forget my father, whispering in my ear, just before I left for New York back in 1967, "you never know son, you might be in the movies someday". He was absolutely correct!

The race weekend was a disaster. On Saturday my 250 broke a fairing mount when I was in 4th place, and I was forced to retire, with the fairing dragging on the ground!

On Sunday, I would have to come into the pits several times, with a mysterious misfire. Every time I did this, the movie folk were all over me. They had 16 cameras around the circuit, and just wanted me and the bike out there, regardless!

During the previous week, I had performed a certain scene over and over again, in the corner called the Carousel.

I was to come into the Carousel, glance over and see Redford standing with his helmet off beside his apparently stricken bike. As I made my way past, I was to look over at him, and continue on in the race.

On the very next lap, I was to slow down from race speed and approach him and his bike, then brake and slide to a halt. I would then lay my bike over onto a straw bale, and appear to run over to fix Redford's (Big Halsey) bike. As soon as it was fixed, he would leap on his silver number 10 bike. I would then give him a shove, and he would take off, and subsequently win the race. All at my (Little Fauss) expense.

I did this so many times, Redford did it just once, I was becoming delirious with the 100 degree heat, before it was finally over.

"When I watched the movie for the first time, I was stunned........"

When I watched the movie for the first time, I was stunned to see that this piece had been cut. All that work for nothing.....that's Hollywood folks!

The season was almost over, the 125 project was nearly finished, and I had teeth again, even although they were false. I was also a member of the Screen Actors Guild now, and Jean had met Robert Redford in person, life was good!

I was about to embark on my quest to win the AFM championship in 1970. Throughout the season it would be necessary to ride bikes in every Grand Prix class, which was 50cc, 125cc, 250cc, 350cc and perhaps in the 500cc, if I

Team owner Harry Hunt

could come up with a decent bike.

I borrowed a Honda CR110 50cc, from Ken Harvey in Richmond, California. I think it revved to 12.000rpm, with an 8 speed gearbox.

Then I had Harry Hunt's 250 and 350 Yamaha's. Our 125 was not ready yet, so I sometimes rode an occasional 750cc Norton Atlas in Open G.P. All of these rides in one day.

It was tough to remember the shift patterns of the different bikes, and I often came in during practice, stepping off one bike, and right away hopping on another waiting machine. As I pulled away in first gear, I was always trying desperately to make sure I shifted the right way en-route to second gear!

1970 was a tough injury year, I had a couple of horrendous crashes, both caused by third parties. But I only sustained minor cuts and bruises, no broken bones!

Harry Hunt caused one at VacaValley Raceway when he forgot to lock-wire the carburetor slide retaining rings, and the slides popped out of the carb bodies. It happened during the opening laps, and I had no choice but to run off the track into the tall grass, or plough into the spectators, I chose the grass….yikes!

The next crash was in Orange County, an infamous back marker named Barry Provisor, who I was about to lap, suddenly fell off his bike, about a hundred yards ahead of my rapidly approaching 350 Yamaha. It looked as though I would miss him and his bike, so I stayed under the bubble as I approached this very fast right hand bend.

At Orange County that year, while leading the 250 Castrol GP, my exuberance got the best of me and I crashed near the end of the race!

As I peeled into the bend, I was confronted, for that fearful split second you get before impact, with the specter of his machine, rolling along rider-less. I hit it dead center, and was instantly catapulted.

Harry Hunt was at this corner watching, and he said I was at least 20 feet in the air, and traveled over a hundred yards, taking down a row of newly planted saplings, which slowed me down quite a bit. My next stop would have been an R.V. parking lot, where I am sure I would have been killed instantly.

The two bikes looked like they had been welded together, bent around each other, and totally mangled.

"Harry was laughing and saying how happy he was that I was alive. He would just have to buy another 350!"

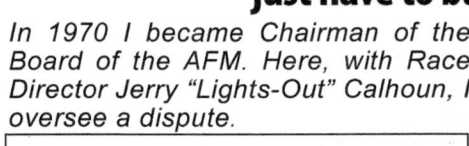

In 1970 I became Chairman of the Board of the AFM. Here, with Race Director Jerry "Lights-Out" Calhoun, I oversee a dispute.

Harry was laughing and saying how happy he was that I was alive. He would just have to buy another 350!

Barry Provisor was not the least bit amused, he was a privateer with very little money to spare, but he did eventually get another bike. Sadly he was killed at Riverside Raceway later in the year.

In 1970, I had been elected

to the board of directors of AFM, and would attend the FIM congress in Cannes, France. Beginning on October 19th until the 24th, however, I would have to be back in San Francisco for the last points race on Sunday October 25th.

Harry Hunt had arranged for me to be met at Nice airport by Jack Findlay and Nanou. She was from nearby Saint Raphael, where she had a lovely old house.

These were the difficult days of Grand Prix racing. The riders were getting a raw deal from most of the organizers, so a few rebellious riders were planning to deliver an ultimatum to the delegates at the Congress. I said I would be happy to hand deliver it for them. What did it matter to me, I lived in California.

Needless to say, this was a big political mistake. I was barred from entering the actual Congress, and spent the next four days trying to explain, and hopefully convince, the FIM that I was not a big time U.S. attorney representing the rebel European riders.

I had to get back to California now, and I was scheduled to arrive at SFO at 9p.m. on Saturday October 24th. I was flying from Nice to Lisbon, Portugal, then to New York and finally to SFO.

Friends told me later that my close opponents were keeping their fingers crossed that I wouldn't make it back in time!

I was home in Walnut Creek by 11pm on Saturday, the night before my final points race of the year. I felt good, so Jean and I had a drink or two.

We couldn't see much point in going to sleep. I would have to leave for the race at 6a.m., so Jean and I stayed up all night and partied, after all, I had not seen her for a whole week.

I could see the disappointment written on the faces of my competitors. We were very close on points, the closest being Jim Deehan.

Kenny Roberts, with his manager Jim Doyle (left) at the very early stages of his road racing career.

I won the 250cc G.P. race, was second in the 50cc G.P., and I won again in the 350cc G.P.

In the 500 G.P., as a point of interest, young Kenny Roberts finished second on a Selby Motors 500cc Kawasaki. His racing number was 479. He was on his way to becoming one of the greatest American riders in history.

The AFM Championship was mine, after a legal inquiry was initiated by Jim Deehan, who questioned the accuracy of the final point score. The man behind the action and pushing Deehan, was none other than Ron Grant.

> "....... Yamaha International refused to pay me a promised contingency of $10.000 for winning the AFM Championship. They ran full page ads in all the motorcycle papers....."

I was not doing well financially, and this was driven home bitterly when Yamaha International refused to pay me a promised contingency of $10.000 for winning the AFM Championship. They ran full page ads in all the motorcycle papers, but simply denied any knowledge of a contingency. I was in despair about this for weeks. I felt betrayed by the factory, after enduring so much grief to win the title. I was devastated.

Jean and I were not doing well either on the domestic front, and after a very sparse Christmas, I made a deal with a charter flight group to fly Jean and the kids back to Scotland. I felt that it was best for all of us.

I would stay here, and try to sort out our finances. She agreed to do this. It was obvious that my extraordinary run of good luck had ended. It was going to be tough from here on in.

yamaha – road racing's number one

The American Federation of Motorcyclists is a club specialising in road races. It's members race almost all the year round, on tracks all over the West Coast and against opposition from many of the top National stars. That's why being AFM Number One really means something to us here at Yamaha. Dave Scott from San Francisco used Yamaha TD2 and TR2 production racers to top the 1970 AFM National Points Championship. A wise choice for Dave who used his riding skills to prove to the rest of the opposition that Yamaha IS a better machine!

Yamaha...it's a better machine.

Here I was, number one racer in California, yet I was almost flat broke!

I stopped in to the Walnut Creek Kawasaki dealership to buy the weekly Cycle News. It was mid January. The owner greeted me and asked me to meet a guy who was with him in the showroom. His name was Skip, and he was the account rep for the Contra Costa Times newspaper.

We chatted about me being a bike champion, and he asked me if it paid big money. I laughed and said that it was so lucrative that I was needing to find a job, and fast!

He had mentioned my Scottish accent earlier, but suddenly he became animated. "I have the perfect spot for a guy like you Dave", he said.

He asked me if I knew where Geissler's British Motors was located, and I said yes. They are one of my clients said Skip, and desperately need a salesman. You with the accent, would be a perfect match.

"won the 250cc G.P. race, was second in the 50cc G.P., and I won again in the 350cc G.P."

350cc Yamaha TR2

And he told me that Al Geissler was also a motorcyclist. Please go and speak to him, would you do that Dave?

I said I would, but really never intended to. I could not see myself selling cars for a living, but Skip had already called Al Geissler, and Al called me at home that evening.

He knew I was Davie Scott the AFM champion, and he was super enthused about meeting me, even if I didn't want to work at the dealership. He wanted me to at least meet his brother Lou.

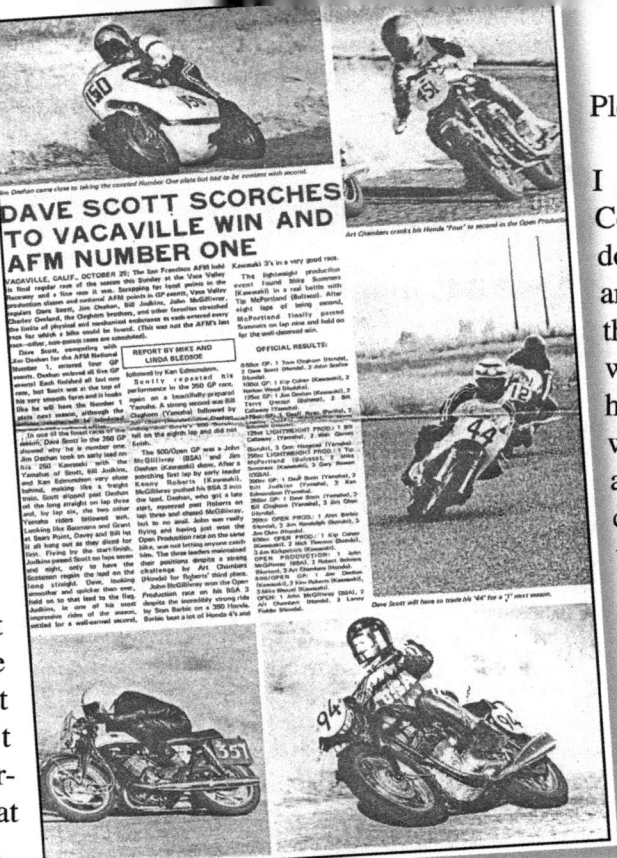

I gave in, and reluctantly agreed to meet at their dealership the next day. So, I would take a look at least, why not?

Al was a vibrant, outgoing kind of a guy. It was easy to like him right away. Lou on the other hand was more serious, flamboyantly dressed, looking every inch a car salesman, and smoking a big cigar.

Al introduced me to his brother, who immediately scowled at me and said, I don't think you are the man for this job kid, you look like hell!

I thought to myself, you are absolutely correct. I couldn't work for a guy like you, so let's cut the cackle please. I must have looked upset, because Lou spun around and took off into his office. He shouted for Al to come to him. Al asked me to please wait. I could hear the muffled discussion that was taking place.

Lou and Al both emerged, and Lou said he was going to give me a shot at the job. I said I would have to think about it. They both said that I should be at the dealership at 9a.m. in the morning. If I didn't show, that was that. I said fair enough. Al walked me to the door. My brother is not as tough as he seems, and I think he really likes you. Please come in the morning.

I got back to the house in Concord and fed the two dogs, who were quite melancholy because Jean and the kids had been gone for weeks. The German Shepherd was trying to dig her way out of the back yard, and the Lhasa Apso was chewing on her skin. It was a nightmare.

I kicked back with a jug of Ernest and Julio Gallo cheap wine and pondered the job offer. I had already forgotten what the job paid. The wages and commission details. But they sounded good at this particular time.

Did I have a decent outfit to wear if I went tomorrow? Motorcycle guys rarely have nice clothes, and are notoriously reluctant about getting dressed up. However I did find a few items, of what I thought would look good. I was feeling a little more confident now, but that could have been caused by the wine!

In the morning I drove our old blue Chevy wagon, which was worth about $100, and parked it in front of the Geissler's British Car dealership on North Main Street in Walnut Creek.

Al was delighted to see me, and took me straight into the office to meet Grace Rubino, the manager. She would get me started on enrolment paperwork and the like. She was such a sweet lady and helped me a lot on my first day.

Lou showed up and shook my hand. "Can I call you Scotty?" he asked, I said yes of course.

Then he said, do you know something Scotty, you look terrible. Is that all you have to wear?.....I said, that's it folks. I'm out of here!

He said, calm down for pete's sake. Grace was sitting through all of this, waiting for me to blow my top I guess.

He said to her, make out a check for $100, payable to Montgomery Wards, and he told Al to take me there for some decent clothes.

He also told me to get that old Chevy wagon off the street in front of the store. Leave it at home tonight! Al was starting to show me around the place and eventually took me over to a dark blue MG Midget parked with the top down. This is yours Dave!

Wait a minute Al, I can't be buying a sports car with a wife and four kids, and I certainly could not afford one either. He smiled and said, gosh I guess I forgot to tell you, that you get a demo with this job. All we ask is that you keep it clean. Moses Tally in the detail shop will do that for you, and there is a gas pump back there also. Keep the car filled up. Lou gets upset if he finds an empty, dirty demo. You have been warned Scotty.

"......I was as determined to succeed. I would be the best salesman Geisslers had ever had, and I did. I was with the brothers for a total of six years!"

Al took me to Montgomery Wards and I got several items to wear. I would blend in better now. Could my luck be changing again, would I be able to make myself a British car salesman. I drove around Contra Costa County in my little blue MG till late into the evening. When I got home, I began to study the brochures like crazy. I was determined to succeed. I would be the best salesman Geisslers had ever had, and I did. I was with the brothers for a total of six years!

I called Jean in Scotland and told her all about my new opportunity. I was selling cars and making money again, and I wanted her and the kids to come back as soon as possible. What if I don't want to come back, she said.

She would have to think long and hard about returning. I was not surprised. We had it tough before she went back to Scotland, but I wanted them all back with me. I assured her that we were coming out of the past miserable existence now. She finally said yes, and came back home to California.

At last, we were a family again.

Skip at the C.C. Times and the Geissler brothers had

Cotati • Kawasaki H1R

Laguna Seca's Corkscrew Kawasaki H1R

Maiden voyage of Dunsco 125 prototype

thrown me a life line, and a new chapter was beginning in my world. I was about to begin a very successful career in the import automobile business, who would have thought?

It was 1971, and I was still riding well, although much less seriously. I was gainfully employed full time now, and had to get used to putting my job first, so I was mainly riding our 125 Dunsco. I refused to enter this bike as a Yamaha, because they had short changed me when I won the AFM Championship. Why should they claim any association with this bike. Dunsco is the association of engineers Duncan and brothers' Scott.

This little bike simply outran all other 125's in California. How often I wondered, how it would have faired back in Europe. But that was just an impossible dream.

Kawasaki USA had just announced that they were going to build a handful of H1R 500cc production bikes. They would only be allocated to riders approved by Bob Hansen, the current racing manager at Kawasaki.

I was approached in January 1971 by a man named Bob Fisher, who was a PanAm pilot, just like the other PanAm pilot, Jim Doyle, who had jump-started young AMA Amateur Kenny Roberts' career.

I had first met him at Kawasaki in Dublin, California, a few years earlier, and got along well with him.

He was itching to get into racing as a sponsor/team owner like Doyle, but needed the right connections. He asked me if I could get one of these H1R's for him to own, and me to race?

I was never quite sure if Bob Fisher was dreaming of emulating the unique saga of Jim Doyle and Kenny Roberts, perhaps with me as his rider. That would be a major stretch of the imagination, but I always liked dreamers, for I was one of them too!

I told him that I knew Bob Hansen quite well. He was the American Honda race manager who had won the Daytona 200 with Dick Mann riding, and got fired for doing that very thing. Hansen had told me the whole tale in detail!

"It is impossible to skip past this incredible story,....."

It is impossible to skip past this incredible story of how Bob Hansen lost his job at American Honda. This is the way Bob Hansen told it to me!

When Honda Japan launched the 4 cylinder CB750 in late 1969 it caused a sensation in the motorcycle world, especially amongst privateer racers.

Hansen was instantly bombarded by riders who wanted to buy race kits, and any tuning data they could get, hopefully to replicate the fabulous factory fours such as ridden by Mike Hailwood. Sadly there was nothing available at this time, and Bob told them so.

At the same time, Bob realized that Honda were facing a big problem. Here was this frenzy of CB 750 owners, attempting to make this standard bike a race bike, and most of them were thinking about entering the Daytona 200 in March the following year!

Bob correctly concluded that all of these private entries would fail miserably, and promptly sent a Telex to Japan, explaining what was happening here in the American racing world.

Honda responded cryptically that they did not need to race to sell CB750's, and did not encourage racing the CB750. They also had no plans to sell race kits or tune up items!

Emphasizing, in his opinion, that the only way to prevent Honda losing face and prestige, was to enter an official Honda factory rider, or a team of riders, he sent off another Telex to Japan.

The response was quite similar. Honda does not need to enter an official team in the Daytona 200..stop!

Hansen's final, bold effort said curtly, "Then Honda will be beaten in the 1970 Daytona 200"..stop!

It was several days before he heard from Honda Japan. The message was this, "Honda Japan will enter the 1970 Daytona 200 with an official factory team of three European riders, consisting of Ralph Bryans, Tommy Robb and Bill Smith. Please make all necessary arrangements. The team will be headed by renowned Honda ex-F1 engineer Yoshiro Nakamura.

Hansen was delighted of course, but also wanted an American rider. After a lot of back and forth exchanges, he was granted just one American rider, and he chose Dick Mann.

The factory three man team and technicians were grouped at one side of the garage, while Bob and Dick Mann were on the other side. Nakamura did not want anything to do with the American effort, and stayed clear of Hansen.

Hansen was in his own right, a well known tuner of British Matchless G50 racing bikes, and a shrewd engineer, before joining American Honda, so he went about the preparation of the bike allocated to him by Nakamura.

Early in the practice sessions, Bob was routinely changing the oil, when he noticed small flecks, or particles, of what looked like rubber. He immediately stripped the engine, and quickly discovered that the cam chain tensioner had a rubber pad on which the chain ran, and it was breaking up, hence the particles, which Bob correctly surmised would eventually block oil passageways, and the engine would seize!

He never consulted Nakamura about this, instead he went down into town, and found a machine shop, where he fabricated a replacement chain tensioner pad, in an alloy material.

The rest is history. None of Nakamura's bikes finished for a variety of reasons, and Dick Mann cruised home to victory.

Nakamura and his technicians put on a brave face at Victory circle, being accorded, after all, the accolades, on behalf of Honda Japan. The four bikes were hurriedly shipped off to Japan after the tech. inspection.

It was rumored that they had titanium frames, instead of the standard steel frames required by AMA rules. Hansen's modification was not discovered, until the bikes were stripped at the factory in Japan. Bob had never told Nakamura how his bike had gone the 200 miles!

However, Nakamura said to Hansen, just as he was getting on his flight home, "Hansen san, Nakamura has learned one thing, that we do not need Europeans to win races"….."Goodbye".

Bob Hansen and Dick Mann decided to take a short break to the nearby Bahamas, to relish the great win at Daytona. One week later, they each went their separate ways, Bob to L.A., and Dick to Point Richmond, near San Francisco.

"When Bob arrived back at his American Honda office, his name plate was missing from the door....."

When Bob arrived back at his American Honda office, his name plate was missing from the door. On his desk was a large cardboard box containing his personal things Next to the box was an envelope. It held his final pay check. He had been fired!

That was how Bob Hansen got terminated for winning Daytona!

Sadly, Bob passed away in 2013. He was a great man.

To get back to the story, I suggested that Fisher and I fly down to Los Angeles and meet with Bob Hansen. I said I would first talk with Bob, and assess the chance of us getting a bike. The cost was $10.000. Fisher said no problem.

Bob was candid, as was his style. He told me straight that he had a brace of top riders lined up, and frankly, he told me I was not one of them.

However, he knew that this bike was a rocket ship, and his First Team guys would either win the 200, blow up, or fall off, in today's jargon, "Win it, or Bin it!"

Hansen however, conceded that he could see the possibility that a level headed, mature rider, might well play it safe by lying back a ways, but still tactically around after the dust settled, in essence a reserve H1R rider, still running in contention. I told him that I was that very guy. He liked the proposal, and Bob Fisher became an owner of a rare H1R Kawasaki, and I was going back to the Daytona 200 in March.

Bob Fisher was almost as new to the sport as Harry Hunt had been. We needed everything imaginable, a technician, a garage to work in, a van, front forks and brakes (the bike came from Japan minus these items), a painter, and someone to make reservations and entries. We had about 8 weeks.

I was not really happy about riding this bike. I had heard rumors that it was very fast, but not too well behaved I would find out soon enough I guess.

Fisher gave me a free hand to acquire most of the items. He would go out and buy a brand new van for the trip to Florida.

My quest to find a technician led me to Merv Wright, a petro-chemical engineer, and a long time racing friend, who lived in El Sobrante, California, and was not racing anymore. He had vast experience in careful preparation of racing bikes. If I was going to take this bike out onto the banking at Daytona, I wanted a guy like Merv working on it!

He was not sure that he could get time off from work (neither was I), but I think Bob Fisher made him a private deal, for he finally said he would do the preparation here in California, and look after the bike at Daytona. Excellent news for us!

The H1R was without a doubt, the worst handling bike I had ever ridden. It literally had a mind of it's own. I was going to have my hands full.

We were in the private Kawasaki garage, grouped with most of the other H1R riders. Jack Findlay had one also, arranged via Kawasaki Italia. He said the same thing about this bike, it was wicked! Everyone of the other bikes were seizing center cylinders, except my bike. The Japanese were all over Merv Wright, to see what he was doing to prevent our bike from seizing.

"Merv was an Englishman, with a really dry sense of humor. When he re-assembled our engine, he used something from an old tin can, kept in his tool box."

Merv was an Englishman, with a really dry sense of humor. When he re-assembled our engine, he used something from an old tin can, kept in his tool box.

He would take a pinch of this stuff, and coat the cylinder walls with it, the Japanese engineers were wide eyed, watching this process, and were convinced that this was a secret potion. They had to have it at all cost!

Our bike still kept running without incident, all the way through practice and qualifying, and the others were in total disarray. Merv finally gave in, and told them that it was Molibdenum Disulphide powder, which he had used, with great success when working on his Manx Norton back in England.

I can't say that it really worked, or whether we were just lucky, but it literally opened up a whole new career for Merv. The mystique impressed the Japanese totally, and Merv would end up at Suzuki G.B. in London, running the whole race organization for several years. I never did see him again in California.

My bike did eventually expire mid-way through the race, but I know it was not due to a seizure. Someday I will tell what actually happened. One thing I can tell you, I was so glad my ride was over!

I rode this bike several times back in California and won races on it. It was a much different animal on tight short circuits, but it was still an animal.

At Laguna Seca, California, I rode the Kawasaki in a demonstration day, staged at a car racing event. This was an attempt to bring more spectators to bike races, a low key, no pressure outing for the H1R.

At Laguna, I was introduced by "Ding" Denton, a racing friend, to a nice guy from Hollywood, who was indeed in the movie business, and was all set to go to the Isle of Man in June, for his first visit to the TT, but something had come up, which prevented him from going.

The guy asked me to more or less take his place, but suggested that I actually enter the Kawasaki. It was spontaneous, but completely insane, and he wrote me a check for $1.000, and asked if this would get the ball rolling. I said it would, Why not?

Bob Fisher said it was o.k. with him, so I would have to call the ACU in England, and speak to Ken Shierson, to see if I could still get acceptance. It shouldn't be a problem, since I was after all, the California champion.

But the organizers of this event are very strict, and after a long discussion, they agreed to accept me, but with no travel money payable. This was a blow, but I agreed to the terms.

At roughly the same time, when the news broke, that I was taking the H1R to the TT (this bike was not yet released in Europe), John Bruno, the creator of cartoon character Crasher Burns, asked me if he could join me on the trip. I said of course.

So the project was now set in motion, and I would have to start raising money. Once again I was asking for more time off, and an all clear from my wife Jean.

Bob Hansen at Kawasaki called me for confirmation of the rumors circulating, asking if it was true, that I planned to take the H1R to the TT. He warned me that there would be legal consequences. Under no circumstances was that bike to leave the U.S. Bob Fisher immediately complied with Kawasaki U.S., and told me he was sorry.

I had made a deal to get a package of John Bruno's Crasher Burns posters shipped to the Isle of Man. John was hopeful that they might sell and supplement or offset the cost of his trip.

They were all ready to go, it was now or never. I might get a ride from some of the people I knew in the U.K. I told my benefactor in Hollywood that my ride had evaporated at the last minute. He understood, and wished me luck, so John and I decided to go.

The tickets were routed from San Francisco to New York, then to London, and finally up to Glasgow, Scotland.

John had never been to Scotland, so I thought we could visit my folks for a few days, then take a boat to the Isle of Man. It's a short sea crossing.

The Boeing 747 was quite new in service, and was having teething troubles, mainly with engine failures. In fact, most of them were carrying spare engines, slung under the wing. This was the fastest way to get replacement engines to all parts of the world.

On the way to Kennedy in New York, the Captain informed us that we indeed had developed engine trouble, and would be arranging re-assignments of passengers on arrival at Kennedy. We should go to the PanAm desk for assistance.

John and I were switched to a flight full of Germans headed for Frankfurt, Germany. We would back track to London from there. That was fine and not a problem. So we agreed, and PanAm re-wrote our tickets appropriately.

As luck would have it, this plane blew an engine also, but this time it would have to land in London. Fantastic for us, we would get off here, end of story, right?

Not so fast, we would not be able to disembark, and leave this flight. We would have to wait in the airport until another plane could be found.

The German passengers were going crazy, threatening legal action and swearing to never fly PanAm ever again. The Captain finally got clearance for anyone who wanted to leave this flight, could do so. Baggage would be unloaded if needed.

We were as happy as could be, but not for long. John was behind me as we approached the British Immigration officer. I showed him my passport and tickets, and he looked them over and welcomed me back to the U.K. I stepped through the gate and waited for John.

He seemed to be in some kind of bother with Immigration, and I came back to the gate and asked if there was a problem?

The officer said that John only had a one way ticket, therefore he could not enter the U.K. I said that this could not be, because we had the same tickets. The officer said, you are correct sir, but you are a British subject and you don't require a return ticket.

"I was floored. John was led away to a holding room, and I shouted to him that I would sort this out.... don't worry John."

I was floored. John was led away to a holding room, and I shouted to him that I would sort this out....don't worry John.

When I looked at my ticket, it was indeed a one way ticket to London, I instantly knew that the New York Pan Am girl had re-written the ticket wrongly. This should be easy to correct I thought, wrong again!

The Immigration people wanted nothing further to do with me. It was all up to me and PanAm to prove, and present evidence of a round trip ticket issued to John Bruno and David Scott, although I was free to go, I had to get both of these tickets corrected. So off I went to the PanAm office in Heathrow. I also phoned my parents in Glasgow and told them I was likely to be late, because of this ticket problem.

John Bruno appears in the background as future multi-time World Champion Giacomo Agostini awaits trackside.

I spent the next six hours battling with PanAm, almost being arrested for losing my temper. Finally reasoning with another manager, when the shift changed. This guy could see right away what had happened, and phoned New York for the numbers on the originals. He reissued our tickets, and I was able to spring John from the Immigration impound room. We were on our way to Scotland at last, welcome to the U.K.!

We had a nice time in Glasgow. My father, Winston, thought John looked like Neil Diamond, and would shout into the department stores we visited, hey girls, look, it's Neil Diamond, and there would be a flurry of excitement. John was embarrassed, but my old man was loving the fun. Winston talked about John's visit for years.

"The Isle of Man was buzzing with the thousands of motorcycle enthusiasts who pour in from all over the world during TT week......"

The Isle of Man was buzzing with the thousands of motorcycle enthusiasts who pour in from all over the world during TT week. We had to find a place to stay as soon as possible, so why not ask a policeman if he knew of any inexpensive boarding houses nearby. He directed us to one called Linacre on Fairfield Terrace in Douglas, the capital city.

It was owned and operated by a Mrs. Kelley, and she said she could fit us in, though her little board-

11 days stay with breakfast and dinner for about $45!

ing house was apparently already fully booked. She was a sweetheart of a lady, fussing over us all the time. We stayed for 11 days, and it cost the two of us a total of 27 pounds 10 shillings, which is approximately $45, for Bed, Breakfast and Dinner....wow!

I had to report to the ACU Race Office first thing in the morning. I would have to let them know that I did not have the Kawasaki with me, and explain why. Fortunately, they were not paying me any travel money, so they were not going to be too tough on me.

SIDEBAR

Current photo of me with one of John Bruno's original "Crasher Burns" illustrations from the early 1970's

Also I wanted to get the word out that I needed a bike. I might get lucky and still manage to get some practice laps in. Every lap is 37.75 miles long, and is a supreme test of memory. I was here in 1965, and felt confident that it would all come back to me quite quickly.

John's posters were here, and he was out trying to distribute them to the vendors and entrants in the Grandstand paddock area. He was having a good time, mingling with the stars like Giacomo Agostini and Barry Sheene, while I was off to see all my old Scottish racer friends, most of whom I competed with when I lived in Scotland. They were surprised to see me again, and we had a good old time. They said I sounded like a Yank now, and I suppose I probably did!

I did several laps on borrowed bikes, but they were not competitive, running well below qualifying lap times. This performance was no good for me, and I decided to withdraw my entry.

The Isle of Man has it's characters too. This is Mose Hutcheson, the "Flashing Kiltie", making his annual pilgramage to the isle.

Ken Shierson of the ACU was sympathetic, and quite relieved by my decision. This circuit is deadly dangerous, and shoddy preparation could be fatal. I thanked all of the people who had bent over backwards to help me.

So ended the trip to the 1971 TT. Bob Hansen was right. Preventing the H1R from coming over here, that beast would probably have killed me.

The other reason, I think he was more concerned about, was that the bike would get sold in Europe. I was offered four times what Bob Fisher had paid Kawasaki, sight unseen. I am sure Fisher would have taken the offer, and Hansen would have gone through the roof when he found out the bike had been sold in the U.K.

".....but he went on to win an Oscar for special effects in the movie "The Abyss"....."

Back in California, John Bruno and I parted company after a short stay at our house in Concord. He headed back down south to Los Angeles. I

SIDEBAR

John Bruno during the filming of Titanic in 1997.

John Bruno was the Special Effects Supervisor on such films as Titanic; Terminator; Avatar; Batman Returns; X-Men, The Last Stand; The Twilight Saga: The Breaking Dawn Part 1 and Part 2, plus many other major films......John won an Oscar at the Academy Awards in 1990 for The Abyss and was nominated in 1985, 87, 93, 95 and 1995. He won the Academy of Science Fiction's top award in 1995 and was nominated in 2007. He was nominated for the BAFTA honors in 1993 and 1995.

would not see or speak to John for many years, but he went on to win an Oscar for special effects in the movie "The Abyss". He created the chrome-like sea serpent that emerged and entered the deep sea diving vessel.

In 1973, the Geissler brothers had a call from the British Leyland head office in Brisbane, California. They were playing host to a visiting Englishman, the son of a British Motor Car dealer somewhere in the U.K. Our Leyland rep, Norm Hotchins, wondered if he could bring him out to our dealership in Walnut Creek and have lunch?

The Geisslers assigned the project to me. After all, I was from the U.K., handle it Scotty!

I gave Norm a call to get some details, like where is his dealership located, and he said, some place that no one has ever heard of, it's on the Isle of Man in the Irish Sea. I told him I had been there before. I knew exactly where it was!

Having a fair knowledge of the Island, and most of the car dealerships there, I asked Norm what this man's name was, and he said it is Mylchreest, David Mylchreest!

Well, I did not know David personally, but I had been in that dealership several times. Mylchreest Motors was very involved with the TT races, and had been for generations.

I told Norm and the Geisslers to relax. I would handle this visit properly, and I went to work decorating the showroom with greetings and a couple of Manx flags, which I had brought back from my previous visits. The main feature was a large sign that read "Welcome Manxman Mylchreest"

Norm had been briefed to bring him in the side door entrance, to get the impact of the decorated showroom, when he arrived. I was amazed to see a young, mid-twenties, tall fellow. I had wrongly assumed that he would be a much older guy.

He and the Leyland rep were staring, open mouthed, at the decorations honoring his visit. David was near tears, as was I.

Thus began a life long friendship. We spent some time together during his stint in California. He was on the last leg of a year long business trip. He had previously been in New Jersey, New Orleans, Los Angeles, and now here in the San Francisco area. This tour was arranged by Brain Mylchreest, David's father, and the tour was designed to give him an extensive overview of British Leyland's U.S. operation, and to hopefully prepare him for the eventual takeover and management of the Mylchreest family owned dealerships and holdings. David had said that he was not sure that he wanted to join the family operation, but a decision was expected of him when he returned home.

Incidentally, he wanted to save the decorations, and I arranged to have them packaged. They would be going back to the Isle of Man with him.

"......We did indeed visit the following year in 1974, and I have been going back there ever since for the last 39 years!"

When David returned home, he obviously made much ado of the emotional greeting that day at Geissler's British Motor Cars, because a few weeks later we received a very nice letter from Brian Mylchreest, thanking us profusely as a grateful father, and graciously extending a warm reciprocal welcome if any of us ever visited the Isle of Man. We did indeed visit the following year in 1974, and I have been going back there ever since for the last 39 years!

In 2007 the Manx Government honored me with an award for attendance of more than 30 years at the Isle of Man TT. I am standing next to the magnificent Senior TT Trophy.

British Leyland offered U.S. customers an overseas delivery program, and Lou and Al Geissler came up with the idea that we could order and purchase two Jaguar XJ12 sedans for delivery at the factory in Coventry, England, which would be sold when they came back to California.

We would tour the factory, then send the second car directly back to California. We would drive up to Scotland, visit my parents, see the sights, and then go the Isle of Man by ferry from Liverpool.

I made all the arrangements and placed the order for the two Jaguars. We had calculated that we could expense all of this legitimately and it would not cost us anything personally.

The trip was on, and we were all quite excited. The Geisslers had never been to Europe before, so this was going to be very interesting for them, and probably challenging for me, as the official tour guide.

On arrival at the Jaguar factory we were told that our cars were not ready for delivery. Lou exploded in a torrent of expletives. This sort of thing might fly with unsuspecting customers, but we were dealers, and this was nonsense, he demanded explanations right NOW!

They had apparently run out of power steering hoses, and would not have any till some time next week. Lou exploded again!

Al then suggested getting a power steering hose from a local dealer, and they sent someone to do this. Could you believe that this was at the factory?

We took the factory tour, while they fitted the borrowed power steering hose, and we were on the road by mid-afternoon. We had barely reached the Scottish border, when the power steering hose began to leak fluid. What could we do now, we were just over a hundred miles form Glasgow.

Once again, Al came up with a temporary solution. We will simply buy a few cans of power steering fluid, and keep topping off the reservoir when the steering began to get heavy.

Listening to the radio on our way north, we heard that there was a refinery strike in Grangemouth, near Edinburgh, and petrol was now rationed. Only doctors and vital services would get fuel, and we were driving a gas guzzling V12 Jaguar, and I reckoned we were in trouble once more as we rolled into the Holiday Inn at Glasgow Airport.

Lou did not share my assessment. After we had checked in, he handed the concierge the keys and told him to get the car filled up. The guy was taken aback, and said that he couldn't help us, there was a strike, didn't we know?

Lou tore into him verbally, saying that the strike, had noth-

I had always believed in sales promotion and this was one of the flyers that I had used to drum up local business.

ing to do with him. He didn't live in this screwed up country, and he better get the car filled up. The guy actually got one of the twin tanks filled during the night. That would be enough for us to cross the border into England, and out of range of this Scottish regional strike.

We spent a couple of days with the folks before heading to Liverpool for the ferry. I had been in touch with David Mylchreest by phone, and he was urging us to leave the Jaguar at Liverpool. He would be happy to provide us with a car, but

Lou was adamant. We are taking the Jaguar over to the Isle of Man. I never understood why?

The Irish Sea was quite rough when we sailed out of the Mersey estuary. I don't do well in this kind of sailing weather, and already felt sick, so I spent most of the trip on deck with my face into the wind. However, I managed to make it without incident.

We were booked into the Palace Casino, but had arrived a day ahead of our reservation, and David Mylchreest was scrambling to find us rooms.

He managed to get us into the Peveril Hotel, which was a bit seedy back then, for just one night. We could tell right away that this was not a very good place, but we would be moving the next day.

Lou would not accept his room, and had come unhinged when he saw it. Al shrugged his shoulders, and went with the flow. The manager finally surrendered his own room to Lou. I decided I would sleep in the Jaguar, after all, we would be up for most of the night drinking and having fun. It was TT time on the Isle of Man!

We were hosted by Brian and Doreen Mylchreest at the family home, named Ballagery House, located in the village of Glen Vine, a wonderful new experience for us. They would come to California several times in future years, and we became fast friends.

Brian and David were part of the team of drivers, who opened and closed the public roads before and after racing. We were privileged to accom-

Brian and David Mylchreest on the cover of the old Manx Airline Magazine

pany Brian on one of these fast laps. It was fantastic for me, but Lou and Al were petrified, especially Lou, who for once in his life was forced to keep his mouth shut. He realized that Brian was a very important Manxman, so he endured his fear.

The week on the Island passed very quickly, and soon we were back in Walnut Creek. I was worn out from performing the duties of the tour guide, and I simply called it quits when we arrived back at the dealership. I needed separation from the brothers Geissler. Al understood I think. Lou did not even try.

"It was over between us. I went to work for a competitor right away, but it only lasted a few weeks before I was wooed back to the British dealership......."

It was over between us. I went to work for a competitor right away, but it only lasted a few weeks before I was wooed back to the British dealership, and we all lived happily ever after, at least for the next four years!

One of the most memorable and hilarious event during my term at Geisslers took place shortly after the brand new Mazda dealership opened directly across the street from Geisslers.
All during the construction period, the architect had deliberately built around a magnificent mature palm tree. It had to be 100 years old or more. It was not terribly tall, but huge in diameter and foliage. It was also home to hundreds of starlings. This was their official roosting place!

The Geissler's hosted a party for the dealership at the Sahara Tahoe at Lake Tahoe in the high Sierras. Jean sits in the left front and I'm the "Court Jester" on the right front. Al Geissler is the third on the left with the glasses and Lou is the fourth on the right.

These birds wake up early in the morning it seems, and head out, en masse, to the fields and farms, where they feed all day long.

The owner, Marvin Benn, was sorry he had kept this tree, because the birds were covering his front line cars with tons of droppings, and the cars had to be washed daily.

He had obviously reached the limit of his tolerance, and we could see and hear that he was getting rid of the tree. It was being cut into sections, and a couple of hours later, it was gone!

When the sun began to set, the starlings returned to roost, and discovered that the tree was not there. They circled for quite some time above the Mazda store, and finally settled all over the roof. Hundreds of them, making lots of noise, in what I suspect was a bird type protest!

Marvin was outside looking up, and scratching his head in bewilderment, and we were all watching this play out from our showroom window.

Al Geissler came up with the idea, let's play a prank on Marvin. Why don't we call him and say that we are from the Audubon Society and were currently receiving calls from irate bird lovers in Walnut Creek, protesting the removal of a registered starling bird roost, which was protected by law.

Even better, Al said let's get Dick Lightner, a Jaguar dealer friend in Seattle, Washington State, to call Marvin up, and pretend to be calling from Audubon headquarters in Washington.D.C.

We had moved a few chairs into the showroom by this time and were watching this unfold. We could here the loudspeaker paging Marvin to take a long distance phone call, and we waited.

Lightner was continuously calling us back with updates, and we were in stitches laughing, because Marvin was buying into the whole charade,

Dick Lightner had told him that he better retrieve that tree at once, and somehow reconstruct the thing before nightfall the normal bedtime for the now homeless starlings. Of course Marvin was now pleading for leniency, and said that it was impossible to get the severed tree back. He asked what else he could do to help these unfortunate homeless starlings.

Lightner told him he would have to feed them right away, and we spotted one of his employees jump in a car. He came back in a while with a big bag of wild bird seed and began spreading it. The birds were watching in wonder from the roof, but soon came down to gobble up the seed. They were everywhere.

In a few days the birds stopped looking for the missing tree. Marvin, to my knowledge, never found out that it was a hoax, and we had a jolly good time witnessing the whole episode. The moral to this story is, make sure it is o.k. to cut down an offending tree!

An ironic twist to the story of our trip to the Isle of Man was, when the two Jaguars finally arrived in California, both cars were correctly designated 1974 models, but because the V12 model had failed the California emissions test for 1974, they had to be sold as 1973's. This instantly wiped out any profit expected.

"My racing was almost at an end......."

My racing was almost at an end, riding only the Dunsco 125 prepared by my brother Jack. I was slowly losing my appetite for the sport, and I knew my time for retirement was near. I had started to wear glasses full time now, instead of just for reading. The signs were there.

Sadly, it came to a horrifying end at Sears Point one Sunday morning, when the bike seized, when flat out coming across the finishing line in practice. I was seemingly safe, and sliding on my back in the direction of the Drag Strip, I realized that there were no solid obstacles in my path. I would be fine I thought, wrong!

The bike was doing cartwheels high in the air above me, and I was thinking that it might come down close by me. In fact it impacted right on my chest, breaking several ribs and puncturing my right lung!

The priceless little 125 was destroyed, and my brother never really tried to restore it. My racing days were over for good, I had had a good run.

I really switched off all types of racing, concentrating on the car business. And I didn't even attend the BMX racing series, my two boys, Allan and David were competing in. It was as if a master switch had been pulled on anything with two wheels. I didn't even ride a bike on the street!

I finally relented, and Jean and I began to watch the BMX kids more frequently, urged on by my good friend Floyd Busby, who ran the Panda team and was the sales manager out of Concord, California. They were competing all over the place, and often out of state, and doing quite well.

The years were whizzing by it seemed. It was 1977 and I was now in management. I had been head-hunted by the local Datsun dealer (before

Early BMX days with Allan in the helmet and my long-time friend Floyd Busby, almost always with a pipe in his mouth! Floyd, who was kind enough to edit and handle graphic design of this book for me, was the weekly motor sport columnist for the Contra Costa Times Newspapers for over 24 years as a stringer. We met when he was editor of "Weekend Racer", a weekly racing publication for which I wrote a motorcycle road racing column in the early 70's. The promotional flyer on page 48 is one of our early dealings.

they became Nissan), Dave Geddes, a very good friend of the Geissler boys. They knew he had offered me a great deal, and I was ready for a new challenge anyway. Six years selling British products was plenty. It was time to find out how to sell Japanese cars.

My oldest boy David, now 19, had bought a Honda CB750, primarily to go back and forth to work, but I had heard that he was already running it in production races.

My friendly informant, fellow Scotsman Bill Donnelly of Napa Honda and Yamaha, had seen him at Sears Point, and felt that I ought to be helping him. He said that he had talent, but would likely get hurt, pushing the CB750 past it's safe limit. I said I would go see for my self.

"........I was slowly being drawn back into the sport again........I could not have foreseen just how far this support would go!"

This was the early beginnings of my return to racing, all be it, in support of my boys. I was slowly being drawn back into the sport again. Jean and I knew that this had always been a possibility, and we had said, when the kids were just babies, that if was affordable, we had vowed to give any of our kids our support, which I had never received from my own parents. I could not have foreseen just how far this support would go!

Selling Datsuns was quite mundane, compared to British sports cars. But these cars were very practical, and sold in volume. They were also remarkably reliable, unlike the British product, and I remained happily with Dave Geddes until 1982.

Early in 1982, the local Honda dealer, named Jim Walton, had recently sold the franchise to the owner of Parker-Robb Chevrolet in WalnCreek, named Dave Robb.

The Honda store was really a motorcycle dealership, which had been granted the rare opportunity to also sell cars.

By 1982 American Honda was setting new sales records in the car division, and there was envy throughout the industry. We all knew that they were selling, correction, taking orders, and being delivered like hot cakes, at a price well over sticker price, unheard of in the import car field!

The reason for this was simple. Their cars would run on any fuel, not just the recently introduced, and dreaded unleaded fuel. And they did not have a catalytic converter either. But best of all, the Honda happened to be a very good, reliable, quality product. Most of us in the auto industry could only watch in awe and envy.

I was quite friendly with the general manager at Parker-Robb Chevy, a good guy called Sam Giamona, who often popped in to Datsun to say hello. In later years, after Sam passed away, Walnut Creek named a street after him.

He visited me on this particular occasion, armed with a proposition. Would I like to go to work at Walnut Creek Honda?....wow, would I ever?

Dave Robb, the new owner, and Sam, were both aware that I was familiar with Mike de Vries, the current general manager at the Honda store. We both had raced bikes in the past, and I confirmed that I knew him reasonabley well.

They both expressed a desire to make the new ownership transition as smooth as possible, making no major changes, except one!

The new dealer principal, wanted to bring about some subtle changes, much more along the lines of established car sales practice, not based on the motorcycle style of operation that existed presently at his new acquisition. Do you think you could meet with De Vries and convince him that changes were inevitably coming, and assure him not to be alarmed by this. I had years of real car sales knowledge at his disposal. If Mike agreed to hire me as his sales manager, I would be his right hand man, and guide him and his team through the evolution process.

I was candid with Mike. The alternative, which was standard practice in the business, when a new buyer took over, was to clean house immediately. Give all the employees an employment application and hope that the new boss would rehire you. By law he was not obliged to do so!

Mike was noticeably agitated. He was the king of this mighty little Honda business, which was evolving at warp speed, and here I was delivering an ultimatum. I am sure he must have thought he was heading for some agonizing reforms.

It was St.Patrick's Day 1982, and I was wearing The Green.... green suede shoes, green jacket, shirt and tie, because I was going directly to meet my buddies at Crogan's Irish Bar for Corned Beef and Cabbage. Mike, I believe, was a UC Berkeley grad. He dressed in topsider shoes, Dockers slacks, and neat tweed sport jackets, quite a contrast to me!

"He shook my hand and said, Scotty, if you are coming to work for me, we are going to have to seriously review your wardrobe,......."

He shook my hand and said, Scotty, if you are coming to work for me, we are going to have to seriously review your wardrobe, I said to him right away, Mike I am coming to work WITH YOU, not FOR YOU, do we have a deal then?

It was now 11 years since the last time I had been criticized for my clothes, but no matter, I was about to begin an astonishing 6 years at the new Walnut Creek Honda.

I was the envy of every sales manager in the area. The chosen one by my new boss Dave Robb. He, and he alone, would fashion my pay program, which he did on a napkin at a local eatery. It looked fabulous, if it all came to pass. I was about to make some serious money!

When I came aboard Mike introduced me to the sales staff. There were 12 of them, two separate teams, with men and women. They were noticeably tense and formal.

I quickly realized that this dealership was like no other I had worked in. It was running well, and the salespeople were doing things as directed. But they were not selling cars, they were taking orders for cars.

Some selling did begin however, when the customers were advised that they would have to join a long waiting list, AND pay above the manufacturer's suggested retail price....yikes, what is this, can it happen? Yes it can, and they did pay this jacked up price!

Mike de Vries had successfully trained, or maybe conditioned, all of the salespeople to deal with this obstacle to buying. Some buyers did turn around and walk away, but the majority signed a purchase order and put up a deposit.

They would leave happy, thinking that they had finally locked in a car of their choice and color...wrong!

Whenever the next shipment arrived, customers would be called in the correct rotation, telling them that their car was here, but it was not the color they had ordered, would they take it anyway?

Most accepted this news (ploy?). If they didn't, it meant they went to the bottom of the list. What would you have done?

My main purpose was to gently feed in the new owners operating methods. I had to be sensitive to Mike's existing doctrine, which his entire sales staff complied with at all times, and without question. So quite frequently they would try to wait for Mike, preferring his analysis of their deal. It took me a long time to break that habit, but I eventually did!

DAVID SCOTT
New Car Sales Manager

WALNUT CREEK HONDA

It was around this time that I brought in Alex Roble from Datsun. He was a real domestic car guy with a ton of experience, and I liked working with him. This Honda store was growing fast, and we needed a guy like Alex. He ran one crew and I the other. In addition, I liked Alex, and wanted him to share in my good fortune.

It was a slow process. I shared an office with Mike, and we exchanged many ideas, some good, some not. He was a really smart guy, and he knew when to back off. He simply started to talk about bike racing when we got hostile!

The transition process, to the point where Dave Robb became comfortable, took roughly a year, and eventually there was harmony all round.

Mike was not happily married, and spent a lot of time in marriage counseling sessions, and personal therapy. I did not enjoy being in the same room when he was shouting at his shrink, daughter or wife Eileen. It didn't seem to bother him.

I had been at Honda for about two years, when one day, he told me that he was going to divorce his wife. It would be a clean legal break. She would get very little from the settlement, he told me his attorney had assured him. No house in the Berkeley Hills, no house in Point Richmond, no vintage bike collection and very little cash. I had no reason to doubt him, he was a strong minded individual at all times.

The morning of his divorce court appearance, he was jubilant and came in early to get something. His brief case was lying open on his desk, as was often the case, and I noticed his Walther PPK 9mm. He always carried the little pistol, so I was used to seeing it.

He took off to attend the hearing, and that was the last I saw of Mike de Vries!

At about 11am. A total stranger burst into my office and said to me, stay right there pal, and I said, who the hell are you? He said he was a detective, and he wanted to know if a certain Mike de Vries worked here. I said yes, he sits right there at that desk.

Has he been here in the last few minutes, he asked, I said no. And asked him again, what is going on?

It seems that Mike had just shot and killed his wife Eileen, and was on the run. The police were waiting at every address to capture him. I was shocked beyond belief, and I thought about that expression I often used when something really bizarre took place, "only in America". I know I have used this expression elsewhere in this book.

Mike had apparently lost out badly in the divorce hearing. Eileen had been awarded almost everything. It was too much for him to absorb, and he snapped. Game over for Mike, and poor Eileen. 15 years to life was the eventual sentence. I would keep in touch with him throughout his prison life however. I always had a soft spot for the guy.

As a direct result of this horrible incident, Alex Robles and I had to go to Oakland for psychological screening and mental evaluation. Dave Robb was taking no chances, that perhaps either one of us might also flip out, and kill someone.

".....Jean and I had formed a small business enterprise named Sport Video International, hopefully to supplement the cost of running the race team."

Our racing stable was slowly expanding. Jean and I had formed a small business enterprise named Sport Video International, hopefully to supplement the cost of running the race team. It never did make any money.

Because of my many annual visits to the Isle of Man, I had made an agreement with Peter Duke, of Duke Marketing, a Manx company based in Douglas, Isle of Man. Duke produced high quality video tapes, mostly of Grand Prix race cars and Motorcycles, but he also marketed vintage prints, posters and audio tapes. We became the importer for California.

Peter Duke was also the son of the great Geoff Duke OBE, the British racing icon of the fifties., who was 90 years old in 2013.

Now we had added a motor home/display vehicle, a Ford van, a video business, and three or four race bikes.

Allan was now 17, and raring to get a 125 ride, and Dave, now 24, had a 250 Yamaha, a genuine race bike. He was doing well, posting a 7th place at Laguna Seca, a 6th at Sears Point, a 4th at Brainerd, Minnesota, where he qualified on the pole.

We let Allan loose for the first time at Riverside Raceway in Southern California aboard a Honda 125 MT. The rest is history He would go on to place 3rd in the 1983 AMA Amateur 125 class at Daytona, and later would win the AFM 125 championship, sweeping the board at Willow Springs, Sears Point and Riverside. It was fun to see such raw talent developing.

In 1984, he moved up to a 250 Yamaha. In addition, he would still race his faithful Honda MT125. But I had a gut feeling that Allan had much more potential, and I began to ponder how to develop him further. He could go to SuperBikes here in America, but I had little knowledge of this branch of racing. I did know about Europe however, and I began to give this some serious thought.

Bob Garrison, a fellow Isle of Man enthusiast, was hounding us to sell him Sport Video International, and I was giving this idea some serious thought. We could come up with a tidy amount of cash, if we sold the business.

I was going to the TT again soon, and I would fish around over there and maybe connect with someone.

Why not explore the possibilities of taking Allan to the 125 World Grand Prix series. *He was now the seeded 125 rider in America after all!*

AMA National #3 Certificate

1983 - Willow Springs - First season

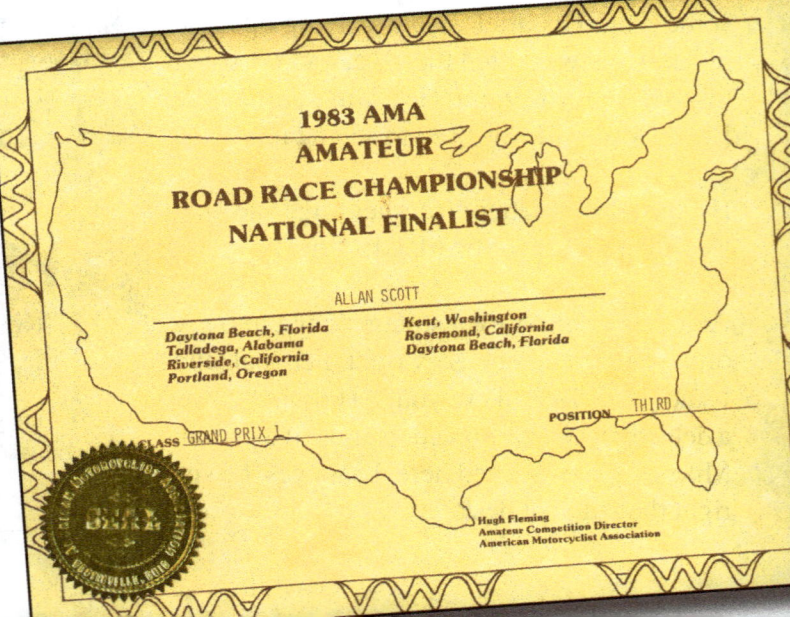

Chris Hughes Brother Jack Colin Scott (Jack's son)   *Allan   Me   Dave Scott Jr.*

1983 Daytona - National Amateur Sportsman 3rd Place Award

EMC 1987

The Dr. Joe Ehrlich Saga

On the grid at the British Grand Prix at Donington Park. Dave Hickman, brother Dave Scott, Allan and EMC crewman.

The story began much earlier than 1987 when I was first introduced to the Doctor by my long time friend and fellow motor trade member Manxman Brian Mylchreest. I knew of Joe Ehrlich's background and illustrious history in the sport, so I was able to converse fairly well with him, and as a result I always made a point of visiting him during my annual Isle of Man visits. He almost always ran a rider in the TT.

In 1986 back in California, my youngest son Allan had recently begun to make a name for himself when he won the American Federation of Motorcyclists (AFM) National Championship in the 125cc class and finished third in the American Motorcyclists Association's (AMA) 125 Sportsman/Amateur class at Daytona. This basically meant that he was now the seeded rider in America in this class, and would be accepted for World competition by the World governing body, the Federation International Motorcyclist (FIM) in Geneva, Switzerland, if he wished to apply?

I had previously won the California based AFM Championship in 1970, and carried the number one plate overall in 1971, so I knew from experience how tough it was to succeed in the sport of road racing.

But the statistics were unavoidable, Jean and I had always said…"If we ever produced a youngster who was talented in any field of endeavor, we would have to give it all we had to bring on this talent, so we decided to do just that for our son Allan, and I said to Jean, let's find out just how good he is.

It was very easy for me to reflect on my own early days racing in Scotland, the incredible struggle it was to fund my career, and with no help from anyone.

There was no money within my family. My parents were hard working class folk who barely made ends meet from week to week, so my racing was not supported by anyone but me initially.

If I had not had the good fortune to emigrate to California in 1967, this story would not have been written, but that is a whole different yarn.

There was never any hesitation on my part to get behind this kid, we could afford to take a flyer on him.

I held a really terrific job for six years as a Sales Manager in a top Northern California Honda car dealership, Jean was an Electronics Technician for a similar number of years. Between us we grossed well into six figures annually.

After lots of soul searching we decided to get the ball rolling. I would begin the preliminary research into how we could get Allan into the 125 World Championship, but at this early stage I knew it would be foolish for me to quit Honda. I knew the racing ropes and was confident that I would come up with some kind of plan that would work. Fundamentally I also knew that money talks. If you have money you can do almost anything.

Sending Allan overseas for the first time in his life with a van, a pair of bikes and a mechanic, was financially quite feasible, but not realistic. I was convinced that joining the GP circus as a rookie in this manner would be disastrous.

My next option was to explore the possibility of buying into a contract with a team already based in Europe, one with a decent reputation and the potential to develop a new rider such as Allan.

1987 would be the last year for twin cylinder 125's. In 1988 the new formula would limit all machines to one cylinder and a six speed gearbox.

"I wondered who was developing new 125 singles for the new formula?"

I wondered who was developing new 125 singles for the new formula? The answer was of course that everyone was working on the new rules!

In England Dr. Joe Ehrlich was already running ads offering what he claimed were competitive EMC/Rotax based bikes, designed to specification for competition against the twins in the last season of 1987.

I was headed once again for the Isle of Man TT in June 1986, and would try to meet with the Doc, run my project past him and see if there was any interest?

No one had heard of Allan, especially Dr. Joe, and he almost died laughing when I told him I was going to enter him in the 1986 British Grand Prix in August!...all we needed was a bike!

He said to me….."If you can get an entry for that race, you must be a bloody genius, but I will build you a bike if you do."

I told him he had a deal if the entry was accepted. How could I lose? If the experiment was a disaster, we would simply withdraw back to California. But what if Allan performed beyond expectation?

The formidable Dr. Joe Ehrlich and his associate Stan Taylor in front of the infamous team trailor.

While at the TT, I spoke with the Auto Cycle Union (ACU) senior representative Ken Shierson, who knew me when I lived in the UK prior to emigrating to California.

As the British Grand Prix was his (ACU) premier event, I told him of my plans and he said there was no problem at his end. All that was required was an FIM license and clearance from the rider's home governing body, in this case the AMA to compete at Silverstone. It was looking like Allan was technically in the British event!

I told Joe to get a bike prepared and I went directly

to Barclay's Bank in Douglas, Isle of Man, and got him a cheque for the EMC 125. The Doc was truly blown away that I had actually pulled off the entry as promised. Frankly I was too!

After the TT I returned home to Pleasant Hill with the news that Allan was going to Silverstone for the British Grand Prix and would be riding for Dr. Joe Ehrlich. Allan, Jean and the rest of our family, and the small group of devoted backers were also over the moon to say the least.

From June till August Dr. Joe and I kept up a good line of communication. He gave me regular reports and was always asking when Allan would be coming over. Would he like to test somewhere before the GP for example?

My stepmother Betty still lived in Glasgow, Scotland, and I put her on stand-by to drive Allan to Silverstone. It was entirely possible that I would not be able to go with Allan to the race, so I asked her if she would chaperone him?

I also asked Allan's older brother David, who was in his own right a well established racer in the States, if he would look after Allan at Silverstone, and he agreed. It was all coming together quite nicely.

A call to Manx Leathers in Douglas, Isle of Man, with Allan's measurements, produced a nice set of white one piece leathers.

August arrived and Allan met the Doc for the first time. Joe immediately set about dialing Allan in to the characteristics of the rotary valve EMC 125. The Doc takes no prisoners when conversing. It's either his way or nothing, and I think Allan was probably not very happy with the gruff way Joe treated almost everyone, but he got on with the job at hand.

Bearing in mind that the field consisted of twin cylinder bikes, amazingly the little EMC single piloted expertly by Allan, narrowly missed the qualifying cut by a mere few tenths of a second!

After qualifying ended Dr. Joe was mighty impressed and tried everything to convince the organizers to let Allan into the race, trying to point out that he had come such a long way to just miss the cut by a gnat's whisker. They wouldn't budge and said no!

At Silverstone in 1986, just missed qualifying!

The next event on the tour was the Swedish TT at Anderstorp the following weekend. Joe implored Allan to come to Sweden and ride for him.

He called me at home and begged me to order Allan to go with the team to Sweden. I couldn't order him to do that so Allan flew back to San Francisco. I did however wish he had ridden in Swedish TT. It was far less of a horsepower circuit than Silverstone, and would have suited the EMC better. Dr. Joe and I both believed that he would have done well at Anderstorp.

However, Joe was well and truly convinced that in 1987, Allan Scott, EMC and the single cylinder format, would be a competitive development team, up to speed when all bikes would be singles in 1988. Joe reminded me that it would also be beneficial to Allan to get a full season under his belt. Did I want to talk contract perhaps?

One of Joe's older bikes. Dave Scott photo

"The Doc would house Allan at his sumptuous mansion in Milton Keynes and school him on the challenges of being a 'factory rider'".

The Doc would house Allan at his sumptuous mansion in Milton Keynes and school him on the challenges of being a "factory rider". The Doc did actually build bikes from scratch, and would transport him for a full season of 125 GP racing, IF we could come to terms.

Over the winter and up till Daytona Speed Week was almost upon us, the Doc and I traded offers and counteroffers.

I knew he was coming to Daytona to run a bike in the lightweight 250cc class with Eddy Laycock riding, so Jean, Allan and I flew out to Florida for one last make-or-break attempt at a deal. I was carrying a certified cheque payable to Ehrlich Motorcycles in the amount of $20.000.

We watched the race and arranged to meet later at the Doc's hotel in Daytona Beach. So after dinner we drove our rental car to the Ehrlich hotel.

The Doc loves champagne and there was a small "bubbly party" going on when we arrived. I spotted an old friend named Stan Taylor who apparently now worked for the Doc as a general odds body, chief cook and bottle washer sort of thing. Allan and I really liked old Stan.

"We got down to the business of a possible contract. Dr. Joe wanted one hundred thousand pounds payable in advance. I told him he was crazy!"

We got down to the business of a possible contract. Dr. Joe wanted one hundred thousand pounds payable in advance. I told him he was crazy!

My offer was going to be $100.000 payable in installments, the first $20.000 right here and now, and I produced the cheque ......The Doc launched into a tirade about wasting his valuable time, embarrassing him with such a paltry offer.So we abandoned the whole thing and took our leave of the party.

The Doc was renowned for blowing his top, especially if he was on the champagne. Stan showed us out and made apologies for Dr. Joe saying that he knew that Joe wanted to make this deal badly, because the Doc in fact really liked me, and thought that Allan was a very bright prospect.

Dr. Ehrlich had many top riders on his bikes over the years including Mike Hailwood, Rex Avery, Ernst Degner (more about Degner later) and a current crop of good British short circuit racers, in addition he had a couple of top Irish racers for the TT and North West 200, so it was high praise indeed to be considered worthy of a ride on one of Dr. Joe Ehrlich's creations.

Allan relaxing with a Coke.....soon he would be drinking Pepsi!

On the way back to our hotel, Allan and his mother were despondent about the whole business, but I told them to relax, the game was not quite over yet.

Sure as fate would have it, less than an hour had passed when there was a knock on the door and it was Stan.

Once again he started to apologize for the Doc and asked if we could please come back and speak with Joe one more time, I agreed and we went back.

The Doc was very stern looking but asked me if he could just take a look at the cheque if I still had it?.......I knew right there and then we would have a deal, he said to me, if he accepted the dollar contract offer as opposed to the pound sterling offer, and of course the cheque he now held, when would the next payment be?

I told him I would come to the Spanish Grand Prix in Jerez on April 26th with another $20.000, we shook hands and the deal was done!

We drew up a contract the next morning, Allan was happy, the Doc was happy, Jean and I were happy, and old Stan was really delighted and promised to look after Allan for us.

We headed back to San Francisco with lots of work to do. Allan to be made ready for his departure to Dr. Joe's house in England shortly, and me to go out and find another $20.000. I had roughly six weeks to raise the cash!

One of our supporters, a travel agent, set Allan up with an open first class round trip ticket on Pan Am to London, one stipulation being that he had to wear a coat and tie on the flight. This was probably the first time that Allan had worn a coat and tie. He looked real spiffy when we put him on the plane. I felt for him though as he waved goodbye, it was not going to be easy working with Dr. Joe Ehrlich. I yelled to him "See you in Spain son, hang in there".

Over the next weeks there were numerous calls from both parties, Allan correctly complaining about the Doc and his iron fisted way of doing things, and Dr. Joe bitching long distance about Allan's more relaxed California style of living. It must have been hell for both of them!

The first race at Jerez, Spain

In April I flew to Madrid, then on to Seville where I picked up a rental car and drove to Jerez de la Frontera, the location of the circuit. Allan had set me up with credentials and a parking pass at will call. It all went smoothly and I soon found the EMC paddock location.

The weather was a bit humid but I was too buzzed by the atmosphere of the place to let it bother me, and I was overwhelmed to see Allan again.....does it get any better?

After all the greetings from the team and Stan, I asked where Allan was staying and could I get a room at the same hotel?

The Doc was not here at this point, but Stan took me aside and said that only the Doc and his son were in a hotel. Allan, Stan, two mechanics and Paul Lewis, the 250cc rider were all in the little caravan he pointed to.

I could not believe it and I blew a gasket. Where was Joe I asked Stan? Please go get him for me right away, I was furious!

"When the Doc showed up I tore into him about the living standard of the team, especially of my boy, and I told him that he had better get all of them and me into a hotel by day's end, or there would be no second $20,000 today!"

When the Doc showed up I tore into him about the living standard of the team, especially my boy, and I told him that he had better get all of them and me into a hotel by day's end, or there would be no second $20,000 today! We all returned to the Doc's hotel and were checked into shared rooms, so Joe got his second cheque as agreed.

The race was not very productive for Allan and EMC. He failed to qualify, but had begun to learn what it was going to take to get the EMC single into the main event, currently dominated by the twin cylinder all conquering Italian Garelli twins.

The most positive thing to come out of this weekend was that Dr. Ehrlich and I would have few problems from now on. Both of us clearly understood each other.

The Doc asked me if I would like to come to his house in Milton Keynes to see how Allan was being cared for, and visit his small factory in nearby Northall-Dunstable. I said I would like this.

Joe was in his element at his little factory, showing me the dyno and new projects he was working on. I must confess, I was also enjoying all of this because there was a time I served Toolmaker or Journeyman Toolmaker by profession, though I had abandoned this line of work many years ago.

He showed me his collection of bikes, including the one Mike Hailwood once rode.

I also got a peek at the drawings for a four cylinder two stroke that Joe claimed Suzuki had gotten hold of via Ernst Degner.

The Doc claimed that he helped Degner when he fled East Germany and came to the UK initially. Many will remember the defection of Ernst Degner, who was the top rider for the East German M.Z. factory.

The designer of the M.Z. was a man named Walter Kaaden, renowned for his work in the field of expansion chambers, eventually to be know as "The Kaadenacy Effect". I had the pleasure of meeting Herr Kaaden at the Nurburgring in 1989.

It is a fact of history that Degner stole the plans of the M.Z and sold the whole lot to Suzuki in 1961.

Dr. Joe also believed that his plans for a four cylinder two stroke were stolen by Degner, and became the basis for the very successful Suzuki RG500. Would we ever know the truth?

The house was actually better described as a mansion, quite rustic but palatial, Allan had a really nice room.

We ate that evening in the dining room, which was very large, with Joe at one end of an enormous table and Allan and I at the other. The only thing missing was a cathedral organ playing in the background!

I flew home comfortable in the knowledge that Allan was in good hands, and would soon start to show how talented he was. Since he had not qualified in the first five races of the season, we were all relieved when he finally proved himself by finishing 13th at the wet French Grand Prix in July at Le Mans. Hallelujah!,,,,he had at last begun to qualify!

The French Grand Prix in the wet......

"There was no stopping him now, and the gang at home in California and Scotland were looking forward to seeing Allan at the British Grand Prix".

There Was no stopping him now, and the gang at home in California and Scotland were looking forward to seeing Allan at the British Grand Prix.

Jean, David and I were coming over, and would meet up with Allan in Scotland a week prior to the race at Donington Park. A bunch of relatives were also heading down to England for moral support. I called the group the Tartan Army!

The Doctor was scheduled for another installment at this event, but a slight problem had arisen, and would come to a head in our hotel in Derby. The whole team and our family were in the same hotel as Joe.

Four races earlier in Austria, the team had suddenly become Team Pepsi EMC. Our 125's and Donnie McLeod's 250's, and the team staff were now resplendent in Pepsi livery. They looked superb and I was thrilled that the Doc had obviously hit pay dirt, and I wondered what Allan Scott Racing's percentage would be. Joe was reluctant to talk about it while I was in California, so it was showdown time in Derby.

When I first heard about the Pepsi deal, I called the Doc to congratulate him. No one had ever successfully landed a deal like this. It had to be a substantial one.

He told me how it evolved….his wife visited a local hair salon every week, and had become friends with a lady also having her hair done. It turned out that she was the wife of the Pepsi Cola representative for the vast Mediterranian zone. The woman told her husband about Dr. Joe's racing team, and the outcome was a contract for the remainder of 1987.

I was always convinced that the Allan Scott, California based team had influenced the Pepsi deal. The rep and his wife were both American.

Unfortunately for the Ehrlich team, Gary Taylor and Suzuki GB with American Kevin Schwantz riding, locked in the Pepsi sponsorship for the future. Dr. Joe broke the ice and probably considered himself a guinea pig in the experiment by Pepsi.

However, I believe the Doc was given a consolation support package from 7UP for season 1988 - all was not lost!

The Doc seemed to be talking another language over this Pepsi issue. He could not comprehend my mind set. He now owed me a piece of the Pepsi sponsorship as far as I was concerned. He absolutely refused to entertain any notion of a split for Allan Scott racing, so I told him that he would not get the next installment until we resolved the matter. He said he would sue me for everything if I didn't pay him.

"SHOW US THE MONEY DOC"

My response was simple, take the Pepsi logos off of our two machines and I would consider some form of payment, but he would also be required to pay me a portion of the sponsorship for the time he had already used my bikes to advertise Pepsi.

He flatly refused and threatened me again with a law suit. Bear in mind that the race was the very next day and Allan had once again qualified, so the sponsor would be pleased to have his product out there in front of 90.000+ fans.

"I told the Doc that I therefore had no choice but to withdraw Allan and our bike from the race tomorrow!"

I told the Doc that I therefore had no choice but to withdraw Allan and our bike from the race tomorrow. I would inform the organizers first thing in the morning that Allan would not be starting in the race.

Joe knew that he was beaten. He could not risk an action like this on race day, and reluctantly yielded his bid to collect another payment from me, but warning me that I would still be hearing from his lawyers.

Allan started in the race, finishing 21st on his single cylinder bike. Joe would have no further conversations with me, however he continued on with Allan to the next race in Sweden, where Allan finished 18th. I know the Doc was pleased with this result against all odds.

Unfortunately at the next race in Czechoslovakia, Allan again qualified the EMC, but failed to finish.

In San Marino, Italy Allan qualified only to brake down again.

Photo by Rolf Korrmann in Austria

The final event for Allan Scott and EMC in 1987 was in Portugal, he qualified 22nd and finished 14th in the race, and did a heck of a job on the single cylinder EMC.

Next season everyone would be more evenly matched, and Allan would have a much better chance aboard one of the two Honda RS125R's I had just ordered for him. He had truly graduated from the Dr. Joe Ehrlich school with honors.

"When the season ended and everyone was back in the U.K., I told the Doc to keep our two EMC's as a token gesture of good will......"

When the season ended and everyone was back in the U.K., I told the Doc to keep our two EMC's as a token gesture of good will. He never turned down the offer and I never heard from his lawyers either.

Now I would have to scramble during the winter here in California, and raise funds to pay for the two Hondas Allan would ride as a privateer in 1988.....*But that's a whole new story!*

One other small but annoying thing the Doc did. When our battle was at it's craziest, he called my Isle of Man friend Brian Mylchreest painting a totally different picture of what was actually going on. Fortunately I was able to redeem my good reputation and character somewhat.

In the October/November 1987 issue of a British magazine called Road Racer, the prominent journalist Michael Scott (no relation) wrote an article as follows....*"Lunatic, Heretic or Maniac Dr. Joe Ehrlich"*, etc. The front page also read, "Genius or Joker". That article really sums up our incredible saga with the Doc. But do you know something? Allan and I wouldn't have missed the 1987 season for the world.......*thank you Dr. Joe Ehrlich, you were really special.*

In the final analysis, Allan had moved from 27th to 22nd in the world standings!............................

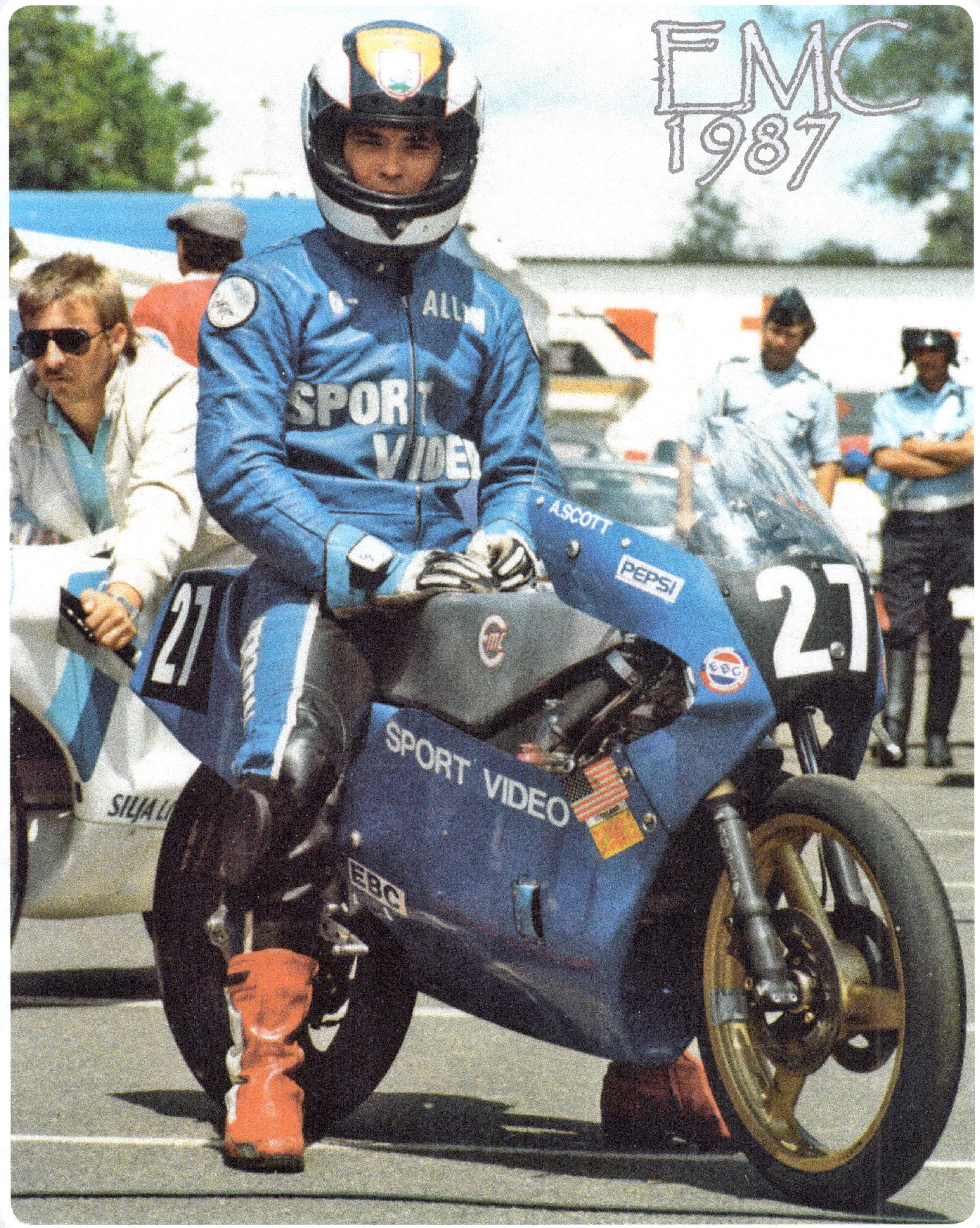
EMC
1987
A.SCOTT
PEPSI
27
SPORT VIDEO
EBC

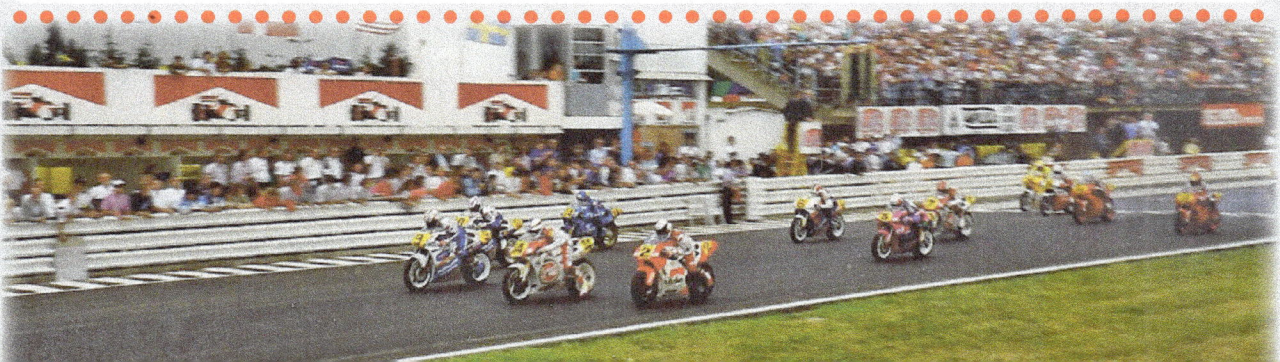

Allan Scott Racing 1988

THE PRIVATEERS 1988

Dave Fender, Dave Scott, Allan, Rolf Korrmann and Jeff Markus.

When we returned to our home base in California at the end of the 1987 season, I began the task of planning for next year, quite optimistic that I would easily come up with a sponsor..... After all, the first race was a long way off, In fact on April 24th at Jarama, Spain……no worries! (I would eat those words later).

I was still gainfully employed at Walnut Creek Honda as a Sales Manager, but I already could sense that upper management were beginning to take an interest in my extra curricular racing activities. It was now common knowledge that Allan was making headway in the World G.P. series, and I was sure they were not pleased with how much effort I was plowing into the project.

They were of course right to be concerned. The car sales business is a cut-throat way to make money. It is ultra competitive and unless you gave 100% every single day at the dealership, your sales numbers would soon reveal that something was wrong. I found it almost impossible and increasingly more difficult to switch off the Allan Scott Racing project when I showed up for work, so I would have to be very careful indeed. The loss of this job would be a catastrophic event for the upcoming 1988 season. If I got fired, it would be game over!

Would I survive until next August when I originally planned to resign?

"Two new 1988 Honda 125's were scheduled for delivery in January 1988."

Two new 1988 Honda 125's were scheduled for delivery in January 1988. They had to be paid for by December 1987, but I was not sure how I would pay for these bikes yet.

Friends and fans were donating money enthusiastically, but none were able to fund the cost of the Hondas, that is until I was able to talk a couple of Allan's school friends into a plan I presented to them.

Joe Olsen and Billy Vassilou would each buy a bike. At the end of the 1988 season the machines would come back to California. They would be vastly updated from standard of course, and the boys could either race them here in California or sell them at a profit!

I knew that Joe borrowed the money from his credit union, but I didn't know where Billy found the cash.

The worst case scenario would be if the bikes were destroyed during the year racing abroad. It was a distinct possibility, but did not deter Billy and Joe from funding the deal…One very major obstacle overcome!

Our racing support business called Sport Video International owned the Dodge van I planned to ship to Europe with the bikes, and it needed to be fettled and painted for use abroad, removing all signage and the like.

I turned the van over to a friend of a friend for this work to be done, and thought that I had overcome obstacle number two…….wrong!

Many weeks into the painting task I discovered that someone, an employee perhaps, had driven the van and blown the engine. In addition it had been stripped of paint and left outside in the rain and now had distinct signs of rust, it was a total disaster!......what was I to do?

The van was a write off as far as I was concerned, and I was getting no where with the paint shop responsible for this. No chance of common sense prevailing. They knew I was not going to be able to fight them. I had no time to pursue them. This was one of the darkest days of my life.

My close Scottish friend Bill Donnelly, who owned the Honda dealership in Napa, California, and had raced with me back in Scotland, heard of my situation and called me. First he offered to come down to Pleasant Hill and help me beat up the painter, but actually he wanted to offer Allan the use of a Ford van he would be pleased to donate!........saved again!

We gave the van a quick plain white paint job and checked it out mechanically, it was pretty sound and would do the job.

I had been working with a San Francisco shipping and freight company for quite some time and had become friendly with their agent Bud McKkellar. He educated me on the best way to get our vehicle to Europe. The plan was to wait for a shared container. This would reduce the cost considerably. The destination was not critical as long as it was on the European continent.

Unfortunately it was several weeks before a client with an older Cadillac showed up and wanted the car shipped to Bremen in Germany. This was our guy who would share the container with the Ford van. We were in business at last, but it would cost Allan the first two Grand Prix's of the new season. He would miss the Spanish and Potugese races.

The van, bikes, tent, tools and everything we thought might be needed were delivered to the Port of Oakland and duly left for Bremen.

Allan and Jeff Markus flew to Germany a few days before the ship was due in Bremen and found a place to stay.

We had budgeted tightly to cover the cost of the stay in Bremen and the amount to get to Italy, but the ship was late and there were German customs problems with the cargo, which kept the boys waiting another couple of days for the van.

When they finally got on the road to Imola, Italy, they were getting low on funds, and they were soon shocked to discover that the Ford was a gas guzzler also. It was going to be touch-and-go to get to the Italian Grand Prix.

They arrived in Imola with less than fifty dollars!

Allan set about qualifying carefully. A non-finish here would be disastrous!.....however he qualified

Allan and Jeff about to take the van and bikes to the ship terminal in Oakland.

American Bob Garrett (left) traveled to Imola to cheer Team Allan Scott Racing on! Allan only had $50 left when he got to Imola!

22nd out of 36 and placed 13th in the race. He was in the money comfortably on to the Nurburgring in Germany. I am sure they had a party on the way out of Italy.

We had friends in Germany we playfully called our European management team, Rolf and Geisella Korrmann. From this point on Allan would have a lifeline if he ran into trouble. They would meet him at the Ring and help him in the paddock if he needed it. I was extremely relieved in the knowledge that Allan could turn to them if he had a problem.

"It was a miserable rain soaked race. Allan was doing well, battling with German Alfred Waibel for seventh place when he ran out of fuel!"

It was a miserable rain soaked race. Allan was doing well, battling German Alfred Waibel for seventh place when he ran out of fuel! Bad luck, but he had at least made his start/appearance money…yippee!

We were all going to meet at the Salzburgring in two weeks for the Austrian Grand Prix. I was flying in with my old friend David Fender of American Honda and Jim Kelly from San Francisco, a supporter of our project.

Allan and Jeff would enjoy a spell in Germany with the Korrmmans.

Dave Fender arrived with American Honda team uniforms, which matched the livery of the bikes. We really looked like a full blown factory team. This was far from the truth and I suspect we may have damaged our sponsor seeking cause. We looked like we didn't need any support at all, however it did serve notice that Allan was a serious contender, and we sure looked pretty!

Allan qualified 24th and finished 18th in the race to bring home another pay cheque. He was becoming self sufficient, which was one more load off my mind.

The guys needed an upgrade in the form of a more substantial tent to work in. They slept in the van quite happily. I set off into Salzburg and found a decent sized tent for them.

Fender, Kelly and I were staying at the Gasthoff am Reidell in Koppel, so we brought Jeff and Allan up there for a good night's rest and a hearty dinner.

The Gasthoff was the hot-spot for the Grand Prix teams, and we had stayed there the previous year when Allan rode for Dr, Joe Ehrlich. We knew the owners and always like to go there.

With a couple of weeks before the Dutch TT, we went sight seeing to a few places I had heard of but never visited before. A memorable one was the Eagles Nest in Berchtesgarten, the summer retreat of Adolf Hitler. Very impressive. If you get a chance, put it on your bucket list.

Another memorable spot was the Zugspitzer Mountain near Garmisch-Parternkirchen, an unbelievable climb by cog railway to the top.

It was a great week with the boys, but they were off to Assen and we had to get back to San Francisco. We would meet again in August at the British Grand Prix at Donington Park.

Once back at work after a three week paid vacation, the atmosphere was tense and my co-man-

*From the December 21, 1988 issue of the U.S. Military publication **THE STARS AND STRIPES** • Column by Randy Barnett.......At the European 125cc Grand Prix races many U.S. military servicemen and women stationed there attended and cheered for the only American rider, Allan Scott!*

randy barnett

MOVING TO MOTORCYCLE RACING, we received a Christmas letter this week from David Scott, who is team manager for his son Allan. Young Allan is the only American rider who competed in the 125cc division world championship during the 1988 season, and he finished 12th in the standings — a fine achievement for an independent who raced with very little sponsorship money.

The senior Scott says: "By finishing in the top 15 of the world championship, Allan is now a seeded rider, and he will begin his 1989 season at the Japanese Grand Prix, then to Australia, then a return to Europe for the rest of the tour ...all of this without a major corporate sponsor behind him.

"Had we been able to strengthen his team effort in 1988, the series of minor mistakes made might have been avoided and Allan could quite conceivably have finished in the top five. Had this been the case, he would now be under contract to a major sponsor."

Alan Scott

As it was, young Scott scored fifth in the British GP, sixth in Belgium, ninth in Yugoslavia, 13th in Italy and 15th in Sweden — all of these hard-earned places good for championship points. Among mistakes his father was referring to was Allen's running out of gas on the last lap of the German Grand Prix while running seventh. We reported at length on that race, one where Allan made a great impression despite his bad luck.

David Scott says that he will be at all the races next season to help his son Allan in his third year on the 125cc world championship trail, a year David describes as the "final push on the road to success."

If you would like to help as an individual sponsor, you may inquire about it by writing Allan Scott Racing, 163 Loralee Place, Pleasant Hill, Calif., 94523.

We wish Allan and the Allan Scott Racing Team all the best of luck during the 1989 season, and look forward to seeing him in action at the various circuits in Europe.

• • •

ager whispered in my ear that the boss was not happy with me. I knew my time was running out at the Honda dealership, but I was not quite ready to pull the plug!

My banker was running scared as well. Someone at the dealership (I had a fair idea who it was) had told him about my tenure being somewhat shaky these days, and he called me in for a friendly consultation. He was worried about my unsecured line of credit. He asked me if everything was alright and I gave him "a thumbs up" and assured him that the bank was in no danger.

Back on the Grand Prix scene, Allan was at his least favorite track, the fabled Circuit Van Drenthe in Assen, Holland, a very technical course to learn and master.

He qualified again and finished 20th in the race. Not spectacular, but he was reeling in the championship points, and other teams were taking notice of him now.

Allan had been to Belgium last season and found the circuit suited his style. As this was the next round on the schedule, he was looking forward to Spa-Francorchamps when he and Jeff pulled out of Assen and headed for Belgium.

He shocked the whole paddock when he finished 6th, by far the most successful

my notice, take the steps to draw out my profit sharing and wind up my affairs in general at Walnut Creek Honda. The cat was out of the bag now!

It did not take long for my bank to react. They called in my line of credit within days, seeking payment in full!........Geezzz!

The irony of this whole situation with the bank was that Jean and I had substantial assets, a nice home, cash on hand, all accounts were current including the line of credit. I knew that there was no possibility that I would abort the racing activities, especially now that it was just beginning to click....What to do?

To add to the chaos, my wife Jean had just been told that the electronics company where she worked, had landed a Defense contract which meant that only US citizens could work on this classified equipment, we were both permanent resident aliens!.....She was asked by her boss if she could comply by becoming a citizen?

A call to US Immigration revealed that it was possible to be "fast tracked" through the process, and we started the application after a scathing lecture for being in the US since 1967 without ever becoming citizens.

privateer at the Belgian Grand Prix. I could hardly believe the news when he called us at home with the result. How I wished I had been there to share his joy.

Allan was getting a lot of press now, and he was gaining respect from other teams. He must surely be on the verge of decent sponsorship at last?

Everything was going to plan with the racing project. Alas, things were not going so well in Pleasant Hill, California.

The pressure at my job was mounting and becoming intolerable, so I decided to begin the procedure of resigning, hand in

Soon-to-be World Champion Hans Spaan hitches a ride from Allan back to the Paddock.

I must make mention of my US knowledge test at Immigration. Jean had been studying with a passion, I had not even opened the manual yet!

Traveling to San Francisco on the BART train for the big day, I asked Jean if I could borrow her manual?.......Needless to say, I flunked the test big time, and got another lecture in the process. Jean aced the exam and as a result of her excellent score, the test officer allowed me **to** accompany her to the swearing-in ceremony.

I wasn't crazy about giving up my British citizenship, and was thrilled to discover that Brits cannot be stripped of citizenship. Our

British passports actually belong to the Queen, and can be used by the holder until revoked by her. Only the Queen can take it away!

We were now a couple of Yanks!.....**HOW ABOUT THAT?**

Back in the real world all my efforts to convince my banker that I was not in danger of defaulting on the loan fell on deaf ears because it had now gone upstairs to collection. It was well and truly over between us!

After a brief emotional chat with Jean, I explained that we had no alternative but to go bankrupt in order to protect our house and other assets, drastic action indeed. We also wondered if this action would affect our newly gained US citizenship. It was a truly bleak period in our married life. Here we were with money and a bright prospect in Allan, and we had to go broke to keep it all functioning!

Allan in the meantime had arrived in Yugoslavia, scoring another terrific result by finishing 9th after a terrific battle for the podium.

I will always remember Kenny Roberts saying to me, "Why did you guys choose the 125 class, it is always a War Zone out there?", I told him that was all we could afford. But most of the premier riders in the 500cc class would gather on race day to watch the fierce competition in the 125 race, especially the American riders who would come to cheer the lone US entry in this hard fought class. Allan was almost always in the thick of the battle at every race these days.

The next round was at the Circuit Paul Ricarde in the south of France. This event was going to be a major disaster for us, during the race and later that day on the way back to the UK.....*read on folks you will never believe this!*

Allan qualified 8th, making him a serious contender for the race the next day. He was excited about his prospects at this track.

However he dropped the bike at the chicane whilst in 4th place, sustaining a horrible cut on his right hand.

He picked up the bike and remounted only to retire on lap 17 with pain and the machine covered in blood (see photo), he was a tough kid to have kept on going.

"Allan had been arested by the local Gendarmes and was in jail!"

I got the usual phone call with a report of the event. Later that evening I was to get another call in the middle of the night California time, mid morning in that region of France. Allan had been arested by the local Gendarmes and was in jail.

He told me that the van, en-route from the circuit to Calais for the crossing to Dover, had lost a rear left wheel.

Blood spattered bike at the Circuit Paul Ricarde in France

Unfortunately it was mid-summer and very warm down in the South of France. Subsequently the grass on the side of the highway was like tinder. A spark from the axle dragging on the tarmac had ignited the grass and it has spread out of control onto a nearby farm and winery. Jeff and Allan could only watch in horror!

By this time many of the other riders in the Grand Prix entourage had stopped to see if they could assist, it was obvious that the van was not fixable, so they started to empty the contents, bikes and tools, into several of their trucks and vans, and would get the stuff back to England at least.

So when the Gendarmes and Fire department arrived, the van was empty.

Allan told me on the phone that the police wanted his papers and money, the farmer/vintner was also going crazy about the damage.

I told Allan I would come up with a solution and call him back, telling him to stay calm at all costs. Easy for me to say....right?

When I called him back, I told him to offer the crippled Ford v-8 van to the farmer. It was fixable for sure, and would be quite unique in that part of the world, possibly even quite valuable. The farmer and the Gendarmes agreed to the deal and were given all the documents belonging to the vehicle.

Allan got out of there as fast as possible, thanks to fellow rider Ian McConnachie who had waited in hope that he would be freed.

Allan wowed the fans at Donmington's Red Gate corner with his speed and lean angle

However, I cautioned Allan that it might not be over yet. There was still the French authorities in Calais to clear….he got out of France without a problem thankfully, and went to the home of Ian McConnachie for a few days to rest his injured hand. Nobody is going to believe this stuff if I ever write a book, I thought to myself!

I now faced the major problem of replacing the lost van. Where do I begin?

With only three races left on the calendar, Donington Park in Britain, Anderstorp in Sweden and the final event at Brno in Czechoslovakia, I hoped I would not have to buy a vehicle.

I called my good friend at American Honda in L.A., Dave Fender, and told him the story. He was scheduled to join me, Jean and the team, at the British Grand Prix in August. He said he would try a few possibilities and get back to me.

Later that day he called me and said that he had spoken to the race department at Honda UK in London. Martin Marshal the manager would find a vehicle for the guys to continue onwards. Just have them get their equipment to London and he would take care of the whole thing. Deal done and dusted!......Can you believe any of this?

Allan and Jeff headed north to Glasgow, Scotland, where we would meet for the first time since he and Jeff left for Germany back in May. It was a memorable time with his Mum and all the Aunts, Uncles and Cousins in attendance. He needed all of this family action to regenerate his enthusiasm after coming through the saga of the French Grand Prix and the inferno. We would hear much more about this fire later in the year and it would continue into 1989!

We will never know if the spell of R&R with the folks in Scotland, or the throng of supporters who journeyed to Dongington, stimulated Allan to the extent that he would give his best performance of the year?

"He was on fire!....Saturday qualifying put him on the second row of the grid in 8th place...."

He was on fire....saturday qualifying put him on the second row of the grid in 8th place. A few of us partied in anticipation of Sunday's Grand Prix. Allan went to bed early.

What a ride he gave on Sunday. Here he was a privateer, challenging all the main factory contenders for the win, taking the race to them on his standard Honda RS125. You had to be there to appreciate his effort.

I was praying that he would realize that his bike was no match for these guys. He was the sole reason he was dicing with the top riders. He finished in 5th place, an incredible result that would net him an additional two thousand pounds ($4.000 approx) for being the Best of British riders entered this weekend, or would he be denied the prize?

He was indeed denied the prize by the organizers, declaring that "Although born in Scotland and carrying a British passport, he was obviously an American, and that Chris Galatowitz was the true winner.

As you can imagine, I would not accept this ruling and protested to the Clerk of the Course Colin Armes. My sister-in-law Elspeth was already at war with Colin's wife Mari and we had to break them up.

However it didn't stop us all celebrating Allan's phenomenal result. The next day we would all split up and go our own ways, Allan and Jeff to Sweden, the Scottish gang back home to Glasgow, Jean and I to San Francisco and Dave Fender home to Los Angeles.

I would deal with the miscarriage of justice when I got home. I tracked down the donor of the prize who agreed that it did not sound right, but that he had told the organizers to administer the award.

Something happened at Donington, because **Robert Fearnall the Managing Director of Donington flew to Sweden and gave the cheque to the rightful winner, Scottish born Calfornian Allan Scott. We felt sorry for poor Chris Galatowitz, but right is right....right?**

In Sweden Allan continued his great performance, not quite as spectacular as in Britain, but qualifying 18th and finishing in 15th position. With only one more round left in Czechoslovakia, it was looking like Allan could finish in the top ten for the season.

The race at Brno in Czechoslovakia was behind the Iron Curtain. You had to be careful in this neck of the woods.

Coming in from the Austrian side of the border at Nickelsdorf, you were told to bring your vehicle into an area like a large barn or hanger, where a team of soldiers armed with

Kalishnikof weapons at the ready, would take your vehicle contents apart. Veteran border crossers would be ready with T-shirts, Playboy magazines and anything from the West, which would be confiscated at once, but you would be free to go!

The first time you do this it is very scary, especially for Americans who were not liked by the authorities, but dearly loved by the people of Czechoslovakia.

The transformation upon entering Czechoslovakia was staggering. Horse and oxen pulling carts and ploughs, old beaten up cars and motorcycles and noticeably poorly dressed children scrambling for decals, stickers or candy thrown from Grand Prix competitors vehicles as they headed for the circuit at Brno. Quite a profound experience for any first time visitor. It certainly made me draw comparison with my early days during WW2. I was eight at the end of the conflict, and children were chasing Yanks based in Glasgow shouting "any Gum Chum?"…..it was as if I was in a time warp when I first experienced Iron Curtain Czechoslovakia. Happily I would return when the people no longer had to worry about secret police and the like and prosperity had come to them.

Some teams took terrific risks by helping to smuggle Czechs over the border on the way back to Austria.

When you woke up in the paddock, which was theoretically impregnable to the locals, there would be people standing around, perhaps hovering about is a better description, eager to trade fine crystal or precision instruments such as micrometers and caliper verniers, for anything you had, T-shirts (old or new), empty Coke cans, magazines or newspapers from our world. Occasionally you would see some of these people being marched away by guys who looked and dressed like G.P. team members, but were actually the secret police in disguise. Very sinister to see this happening. Thank goodness that we never lived under a system like this.

Allan liked this track, which thousands of East

Germans traveled to. Crowds of 250.000 were not unusual here, and Allan said he could feel the crowd willing him on at times.

"He had clinched number 12 in the 1988 World rankings. What a great achievement for a modestly funded, totally private team running absolutely standard bikes."

He qualified 24th and finished in a tight group to take 10th place. He had clinched number 12 in the 1988 World rankings. What a great achievement for a modestly funded, totally private team running absolutely standard bikes.

Happily, the bikes had finished the year in good shape, Joe Olsen and Billy Vassilou's gamble had paid off. They would take possession of the Hondas when they arrived back in California a few weeks later.

This was the most unbelievable year in all of our lives! I had quit a six figure job. Jean and I had become US citizens, then we went bankrupt (only on paper), the team van was now in France for EVER, and we were being sued by a French farmer…..but Allan had finished 12th in the World. How about that for a year?.....I simply HAVE to write a book some day sez I!

Back home once again in Pleasant Hill, it was time to catch up with home chores and such, I was getting calls from various parts of the racing world now, inquiring about the 1989 season plans for Allan. Something was brewing out there for sure, but I went ahead and ordered two new Honda 125's for next season just in case we would be privateers again.

Allan dicing with Gaston Grassetti……

It's been a long season.......

Sears Point International Raceway

Castrol 250 GP

12th in the World
ALLAN SCOTT

Allan Scott, California's top Grand Prix privateer, is home after completing his second World Championship season, a season the team has dubbed...the "What If" season!

The Northern Californian is competing here this weekend aboard a 250cc machine to contest the Castrol 250 GP event, a deviation from the 125cc World Championship that he ran in Europe this season.

With a superb 5th place at the British Grand Prix, a 6th in the rain in Belgium, 9th in Yugoslavia, 10th in Czechoslovakia, 13th in Italy and 15th in Sweden....*What If*....Scott had made it to the opening round in Spain?....and if he hadn't run out of fuel in the German GP while in 7th place on the last lap?...or...he had not fallen four laps from the finish of the French GP while running 3rd?... Just suppose he hadn't caught the flu just before the Dutch T.T.? And imagine the vital points lost in Austria because of a reed valve defect that went undetected?.... What if the team had had adequate sponsorship to buy all of those very special parts available, yet totally unaffordable throughout the entire season!....And finally, what if the tire supplier had always been able to fit the correct rubber compound when Scott asked for it?....and had never run out of those tires at almost every Grand Prix that he entered?

While it was obvious to the racing fraternity that Jorge Martinez and Exio Gianola would be impossible to catch in 1988, the remaining positions were destined to develop into a "free-for-all" battle, and Scott very quickly found that he was one of the contenders who would seek a place in the top group.

It was virtually certain that Scott would have ended the season in the top five, however, the mishaps which plagued the team made it difficult to say the least, and it is incredible that Scott and Jeff Markus, his tuner, stuck with the program. Together they produced a result that can only be described as fantastic!

Scott is not certain what lies ahead in 1989, but you can be sure that he will be back with even more experience, determination and dedication.

Where there's a will......
There's a way!

A feature article that appeared in the program at the 7th Annual Camel Pro AMA Motorcycle Championship Race at the Sears Point International Raceway in Northern California.

1ST lap of the British Grand Prix at Donington Park. Scott, #22, leads Julian Miralles #36, Corrado Catalano #21 (behind Scott), Domenico Brigagglia #2, Lucio Pietroniro #9, and Adi Stadler #20. Scott placed 5th in this race.

Hero Drent Photo

1989
The Year of CORONAS

The season began in Suzuka, Japan on March 26th. Our new bikes were still in basic white as delivered. I had not yet landed a major sponsor, but there were lots of rumors that we had!

I did not attend the Japanese Grand Prix this time, but Allan was in contact with me at all times. He had told me that a group representing a Japanese company named Jyohoku Honda Auto (JHA), were asking for clearance to run our bikes in their livery and to their technical specification. Allan and Jeff would not have to do anything to the bikes, and they would even fit Allan up with new leathers….. It sounded like a good deal to me and I told Allan to go ahead. In addition, Bridgestone tires were going to supply us at no charge to Allan Scott Racing.

Although we used Dunlop tires, we had no contract with them. In addition we had to pay full price for each set of racing tires. I told Allan to accept the deal and have the Bridgestone people contact me with a view to using their tires for the whole season.

The JHA team did wonders for our box stock 125 Honda, a main visible feature being a completely different expansion chamber and a red paint job, all of which belonged to them, and would be stripped from the bike before it left Japan for the next round in Australia.

This was the first 125 race in Japan since 1967 and the local Japanese competitors were riding like demons on their home circuit, determined to show the World Grand Prix invaders, and of course the Japanese manufacturers present on race day, just how good they were. The GP regulars were screaming blue murder about the aggressive style of riding they had to contend with. Allan was quite at home with this issue, because you would never make progress in the 125 class if you were NOT aggressive. All in a days work he said!

The season begins in Suzuka.

The JHA set up produced a fast bike, but Allan barely squeezed into the main event, finishing in 30th place, probably as a result of all the aforementioned elbow and knee banging with the local lads during qualifying!

In the main event the competition was ferocious!

Allan ended up in 13th place and managed to escape the carnage. I think he played this race with intelligence and I told him so....well done son!

The JHA team were very happy too, and agreed to let Allan have a few parts to take away with him, promising that they would be in touch with me to discuss a possible further involvement.

Bridgestone also liked his result on their rubber, and loaded Jeff up with tires for the Australian Grand Prix at Philip Island. The race on the 9th of April would be the first Grand Prix at this circuit. It would also be a first memorable achievement for Allan Scott Racing!

Rod Hurtado, one of our sponsors, joined Jeff and Allan for some rest and relaxation in the Australian sunshine, and at the same time enjoyed the local hospitality of the very friendly Aussie ladies!

The bike was really working well and Allan loved the circuit, learning it very quickly and qualifying in 8th place on the grid. I know our guys were excited and very optimistic about Allan's chances on race day, so too were Jean and I back home in Pleasant Hill. We sat up all night waiting for the usual results phone call, which was incidentally my wish, that he or Jeff make this call home immediately following each race, BEFORE anything else. This was the pre-internet era folks! It is impossible to describe the impact of the call from Australia. Allan was on the rostrum in third place, wow!

We did eventually get to see the race on a VHS tape we received from friends in Melbourne, Australia. I spotted a terrible thing almost immediately. Allan was wearing a yellow Dunlop hat on the podium?

As agreed in Japan, we would run Bridgestone tires in Australia. Allan even had a Bridgestone patch on his leathers in plain sight on the podium!

"The Australian Dunlop representative on the winner's rostrum, had cunningly snatched off Allan's Bridgestone cap and replaced it with a Dunlop one!"...

Practice

The Australian Dunlop representative on the winner's rostrum, had cunningly snatched off Allan's Bridgestone cap and replaced it with a Dunlop one!....after the ceremony, he just laughed it off when Allan protested, however it was too late, the dirty deed was done.

The event was of course being viewed live in Japan, and I was soon bombarded by fax messages from irate Bridgestone tire people. I told them what had happened and begged for forgiveness. I truly believe that this incident cost Allan Scott Racing a deal with Bridgestone of Japan!

The next race was at Laguna Seca in California. Sadly there was no 125 class at this one. What a pity that Allan was deprived of a chance to show his talent to the home crowd, and his small band of sponsors and supporters.

Allan and Jeff therefore decided to fly back to London with the British 125 riders. There were 21 days until the Spanish round in Jerez, and we did not have a transporter yet.

Martin Marshal at Honda UK to the rescue once again. He spoke with fellow racer Ian Newton, who was sponsored by Trans Freight Europa, and they agreed to lend us a Mercedes box van for the season....we sure owed Martin and Honda UK for all their help.

Allan and Jeff collected the Mercedes diesel and headed up to Scotland to fit out the empty box, bunk beds, racks for storage, a small fridge etc.

The man behind the re-fit was his cousin Graham Duncan, an elevator technician by trade, but a keen handyman and carpenter.

The boys had a good time in Glasgow, where all our relatives live, but they soon had to get back to Honda UK warehouse and pick up the bikes and head for Spain.

The Mercedes truck was a plain white unmarked box van, and ran flawlessly for most of the year. Those Mercedes diesels just keep on running!

Jerez is another one of Allan's favorite circuits,

Spanish Grand Prix

and he demonstrated this by qualifying 5th, and finishing 6th after a terrific scrap for the podium, all of this achieved as an un-sponsored privateer.....but not for much longer I suspected!

The race in Spain was also the first time we met Trevor Manley, the Australian 125 entry, who was struggling to qualify at this challenging and highly competitive level. Far more serious than racing back home in Australia, but he was the seeded Australian 125 entry and was approved to come to Europe. We would come to enjoy the company of Trevor and his wife Leslie throughout the season.

Alas Trevor got in a bit of trouble at the British Grand Prix. I will explain later on in the story.

At the Italian Grand Prix in Misano-Adriatico on May 14th, Allan qualified in 15th, but only managed a solitary lap in the main race!

Jeff had been getting visits from Joan (Catalan for John) Jornet, the head mechanic of the Coronas, Spanish team, and it seemed that there was interest in talking a possible sponsor deal. Jeff and Allan felt that I should speak to him at Hockenheim, Germany, which was the next race on the schedule. I would be joining the boys for the rest of the season at this race...I would speak to Joan Jornet at that time.

I knew Allan was going to be lacking in horse-power at Hockenheim. The circuit is a speed-fest with long straights that disappear off into dense forested area, and re-emerge back into view at a section named the Stadium. The majority of fans are in this section of corners in full view of the grandstands.

As predicted, he was out gunned in Germany, qualifying in 18th and finishing the race in 22nd!

I promptly made contact with the actual Coronas team manager by telephone. He was a Barcelona attorney named Alberto Xiol (pronounced Sheol).

His English was limited and my Spanish was the same, so he linked me with a secretary who sorted out my questions and his answers.

In essence, their rider Alex deBon had been injured and probably wouldn't make it back till later in the year. The owner of Coronas, which is based in the Canary Islands, a Spanish territory, was a true bike racing enthusiast who threw parties at his home each and every race day to cheer on his personal entry!

He was urging Alberto to replace deBon with another capable rider, obviously he would prefer a Spanish rider, but no other qualified un-contracted Spaniard was available!

I told him that we were of course interested, and he said he would get back to me shortly.

In another wet race in Austria, Allan qualified really well again in 6th place, and after a grueling, crash infested 125 thriller, finished 9th. This circuit was more to his taste!

He was dueling with the leaders when he slid off. He picked himself up and re-joined the race to fight his way back to seventh, only to fall off again at the same bend. This time he got going again and scorched his way back to 9th on the last lap.

He told me later that it was so slippery out there that he simply turned the bike into the corner and down he went. He could hardly believe that it happened again at the very same corner. We have the video at home and it is always good for a giggle. The fans at that corner enjoyed the spectacle no doubt.

"It was great to be on the road with Jeff and Allan at last. I hoped that I would be an asset and not a hindrance. We worked fairly well together for a while".

It was great to be on the road with Jeff and Allan at last. I hoped that I would be an asset and not a hindrance. We worked fairly well together for a while.

On our way to Assen for the Dutch TT, I called Alberto Xiol once again in Barcelona and he was noticeably excited. The Coronas boss had given him clearance to bring Allan and I to Barcelona for a test ride and possible contract talks.

The Coronas team had two brand new J.J. Cobas Rotax 125's, the exact bikes that Alex Criville was riding currently. They wanted Allan to ride them at Calafat a short circuit near Barcelona. Could we come to Barcelona right away, all expense would be paid by Coronas?

I agreed that Allan and I would come to Barcelona. Jeff would remain at the Dutch circuit until we returned.

When we arrived at the Assen circuit on June 6th in Holland, it was locked up tight and would not normally be opened until around about June 18th when the teams would arrive a few days before the TT.

I found a security man and persuaded him to let us in. We said we would park as far away as possible from view, and make no trouble. The Dutch are really mellow and helpful people.

I went into Assen on the moped and bought the train and airline tickets. We would arrive in Barcelona on June 10th. Alberto would arrange for Joan Jornet to be at the airport to meet us.

Jeff was not complaining. The one thing he really enjoyed was sleeping and he was going to sleep big time while we were gone, and of course he could take the train to Groningen for additional sport as well!

Joan met us and drove us to a small seaside resort town called Sitges, roughly 60 miles from Barcelona, and quite close to the circuit at Calafat where Allan would try out the Cobas machines.

Coronas had booked us into a nice hotel named the Antemare in Sitges, and we took a look around the town that evening. We liked it so much that we would return more than once in the future.

The team and the transporter would be coming from Martorell near Barcelona. Alberto would also join us with his English speaking secretary Lucia.

I began to think ahead, I would need a typewriter to pound out a possible contract during or near the end of this tryout. Once again folks, I would remind you that this was long before lap tops and the like.

The hotel concierge said he would make one available to me if and when I needed it. In the meantime I was scribbling like crazy making notes by pencil!

Joan picked us up in the morning and drove us to Calafat. The Coronas team was already there and Pepe the chef, driver and general fixer, had fresh coffee ready, or a beer if anyone wanted one. That's the way it is Catalunya, perfectly normal to have beer at breakfast time!

The team and equipment looked spectacular and very business like. Allan did a couple of laps on the team moped and said he was ready for the test.

I reminded him that these bikes were rotary valve engines, just like the EMC Rotax engines he rode in 1987, and they would tend to be a bit ferocious in power delivery, unlike the gentler reed valve Hondas.

Off he went for a few warm up laps, and a little later, off he fell at a slow hairpin bend with no real damage to him or the bike.

We were all eager for his feed-back on the circuit and the Cobas 125. He said he was not that impressed with the bike and would much rather be riding his Honda today, but he liked the circuit very much.

During a nice lunch at a nearby beach front restaurant, Alberto and I started to touch on the subject of the cost to hire Allan for the rest of the season. I said it was premature at this stage, but he was anxious to give the owner of Coronas in the Canary Islands an idea of cost.

When we got back to Calafat, Allan asked for a few adjustments and took the bike out again.

The team had the stopwatch running at each session. They also knew the lap record for 125's at Calafat was held by Jorge Martinez, the Spanish World Champion.

"Four laps into the session the team of technicians went berserk. Allan had just equaled the lap record."........

Allan prepares to test the Team Coronas Cobas

Four laps into the session the team of technicians went berserk. Allan had just equaled the lap record. That was enough for Alberto who immediately phoned the Canary Islands with the news.

There was much back slapping and hand shaking when they called Allan in to end the test. Now it was time to talk about a contract, however there was a major obstacle that had to be dealt with.

Allan did not think that he could produce results with their J.J.Cobas bikes. The team technicians were stunned in disbelief. How could he think like this?

I suggested to Alberto to phone the boss again and explain the situation. It would be best to get this problem resolved before going any further with the deal, and he agreed.

The owner in the Canary Islands didn't really seem to care about the bikes, Honda or Cobas, it was all the same to him, he simply wanted to win races!

I told Alberto that I would easily duplicate his Coronas livery and logos, if he gave me the DuPont paint number and sample logos. This I would guarantee to accomplish by the time the team arrived in Assen. Actually I had absolutely no idea how I would get this done in time!

We all went our separate ways, Alberto to ponder the protests of his team technicians, me to the hotel to generate a contract just in case we came to terms. I was up all night writing the key terms of a maybe contract.

The next morning Alberto sent Joan to collect us from the hotel. We checked out and went to Martorell to the workshop of the team. It was a very professional set-up organized by Joan Jornet.

After a look around the town, and a visit to Joan's local bar, called the Lennon Pub, which was filled with John Lennon posters, Joan said that Alberto had arranged for Allan to be measured for a set of racing leathers, just in case we had reached agreement on a contract. He also wanted Joan to deliver us to Alberto's Barcelona office to get further acquainted.

It was a truly beautiful old building, with a caged elevator running up through the center to the upper floors. Alberto was actually born in this very building he told me, and his Father and Grandfather had lived here for generations. They were also attorneys by profession.

The office was grand to say the least, with doors that reached upwards at least 20 feet, very impressive indeed.

Alberto Xiol was a really cultured, quiet yet firm sort of guy, easy to work with, though most talks were via the secretary in translation.

He was rightfully concerned that the non-use of the team bikes was troubling the whole Coronas team, but I reminded him that I was aware that the cost of running the Cobas bikes was considerable compared to the cost of spares for a Honda, and that we had a special account with HRC in Belgium. He was guaranteed to save a bunch in the long run. There goes that guarantee word again!

I agreed on a small concession, that Allan would re-evaluate the Cobas machines at some time during the season. This never really happened because the Hondas were doing just fine.

He was listening intently, and asked me if I had prepared a proposal. I said I had indeed and produced my typed contract.

Alberto also had concerns about the reaction of the Spanish press, which would be inevitable.

"The Scottish Born Californian of Mediterranean Descent"

My suggestion was, if we come to terms, that we make a release worded along these lines…"Allan Scott, Scottish born Californian of Mediterranean descent etc"….he liked it, and the press used it to explain and appease the fanatical Spanish motorcycle followers as the reason why Coronas had gone outside of Spain for a rider.

He said he would have Lucia translate it to Spanish over the weekend. In the meantime would Allan and I join him and his family for dinner at his hillside villa above Sitges.

He apparently lived and worked during the week in the same building as the office, and then joined the family at the weekends.

We were scheduled to leave Barcelona for Amsterdam on Tuesday the 15th June, so we could at least enjoy part of this wonderful weekend with Alberto and his lovely family.

Allan and I were back at the hotel Antemare in Sitges until our Tuesday departure. Lucia would brief Alberto with my contract proposal on Monday. It was coming close to decision time.

We didn't see Alberto until Tuesday at the Barcelona Airport, so I was fairly sure we had not landed the contract.

Joan delivered us and we all met in the cafeteria. Lucia had typed my contract on to a proper Coronas letterhead, with all the necessary and correct signing places. After all they were a law firm!

Alberto was still stuck on the issue of the bikes, and didn't appear to be willing to accept otherwise. He had a little bag on the table with what I assumed were some going away gifts for us, and he handed me an envelope containing the cash reimbursement for our travel expenses, but still no sign of movement on the contract.

They had called the flight to Amsterdam twice when he finally spoke out……."let's do it your way David, sign here Allan, sign here David, and then he quickly signed for Coronas. The bag on the table actually contained the DuPont paint codes and color samples, plus a few sample Coronas logos. Alberto had come prepared and he was smiling!

We shook hands and echoed…. "We will see each other in Assen on the 24th". I was going to be very fortunate to find someone in Holland who could paint our Hondas in time for the Dutch TT, and the arrival of the Coronas transporter. Alberto would also be flying in to join us in Assen.

"Things were looking up for Allan Scott Racing. Allan was finally being paid to race. At this stage it was serious money at last!"

On the flight back to Holland, Allan and I looked over the contract. Things were looking up for Allan Scott Racing. Allan was finally being paid to race. At this stage it was serious money at last!

Arriving quite late at Schipol Airport, Amsterdam, we caught one of the last trains to Assen, then a taxi out to the circuit. We were already wondering how we would get access to the paddock where Jeffrey parked the truck?

No problem, Jeff had moved the truck in anticipation that we would roll in late, and we spotted it almost immediately. It was now close to the fence, so over the fence we went, scaling it easily.

We could hardly wait to tell him the good news, and soon opened up the Heinikens in celebration. What a week this had been!

As I mentioned earlier, the Dutch people are extremely friendly, and we had befriended a local postman named Rudi Middleboss a few seasons ago. He usually stopped by after the morning mail deliveries to chat about racing, especially the racing in the old days.

He lived and worked in the village of Smilde, which was close bye. I reckoned that Rudi was the man who could find me a painter, so I briefed him on the task and sent him on the mission, reminding him that we had just 8 days to get it done. He said he would be back in a while, and he peddled away on his post office bicycle!

Rudi "The Postman' Middleboss and his wife Cristien relax with the author in the village of Smilde.

At noon time on the very same day he returned in a van carrying signage saying…Rekame- Menders, the rough translation is Repair and Fix. The guy was a body shop owner!

He was a quiet chap with no English. Between Rudi, myself and the Menders-Reklame man, I was able to show him what we had to accomplish.

We had pictures of the Coronas J.J.Cobas bikes. We had the DuPont color code and the sample logos.

We explained that it would involve the fairing, seat, tank and logos located precisely where the Coronas team had affixed them to their bikes. He nodded and through Rudi, told Jeff to take the parts off of the bikes and load them into his van.

He told Rudi to bring us to his place of business if we were worried, and he would show us around. We agreed and followed him in our truck.

It is hard to explain how surprised we were when we arrived.

The shop was housed inside a rustic Dutch traditional barn, right alongside a canal. Once inside, it was filled with the most up to date equipment I had ever seen, even a computer generated printer to duplicate logos and decals. Now I was worried about how much this was going to cost us!

All the time he was smiling, I think with pride for his modern shop neatly disguised as a barn, and I think a little bit because he realized, that he alone knew that he was going to bale us out of big trouble. I truly hoped that I was correct!

Rudi of course was delighted and took us to his home in Smilde for beers in celebration once again. They celebrate a lot in Holland!

We had time to kill now, Jeff had replaced the crankshaft in one bike, and the other bike was set-up for rain in event would be a wet race. Both were basically ready to go except for the parts now at the painter.

Rudi took us over behind the main grandstand at the start/finish line of the circuit. He told us we were going to The Flying Club of Assen. I couldn't imagine where there might be a runway. Lead on Rudi said I.

Sure enough, there was the control tower and the main office, which included the club bar, which would become a regular hot spot for us....more celebrations!

You surely must have guessed it by now, it was The Model Flying Club of Assen. No other riders or teams knew about this place, and they literally adopted us during our stay in Assen. This friendship remained the same when we came back in following years.

"……….It was unbelievable how perfect the quality of his work was. I was stunned. I never thought for a minute that the project would be so perfect. The painter was all smiles".

On Monday morning the 19th of June, our painter brought back the parts; It was unbelievable how perfect the quality of his work was. I was stunned. I never thought for a minute that the project would be so perfect. The painter was all smiles.

Now it was crunch time!......How much did I owe him I asked?

He said how about two complementary tickets for the TT this weekend? I easily arranged for Paddock passes for him and Rudi. These credentials were like gold in Holland, so both guys were delighted to get them. I had once again dodged a giant bullet!

As you can see from the photos, the bikes looked spectacular in Coronas colors. I was confident that Alberto Xiol and the Coronas team would be blown away, and indeed they were, but in the happiest of ways!

The team truck was loaded up with T-shirts and uniforms, and Allan's leathers were also ready.

IRTA (International Racing Teams Association) had assigned their paddock parking spot alongside us. When the rest of the teams saw the new Coronas team with Allan Scott, the place was abuzz!. Good things were happening for the Scottish born Californian of Mediterranean descent, yes sirree!

Alberto made his first payment of the contract in cash. I wanted it that way. We were on the road and not set up yet with a bank to handle foreign cheques. Perhaps a little later. We were quite new at receiving money to do this work. Alberto was concerned about bringing real money out of Spain, he was an attorney after all.

He was so pleased with the finished bikes, that he asked me if I could paint the Mercedes box van also. I could not do that because it belonged to Trans Freight Europa in the UK.

Pepe made dinner for all of us that night, and we ate under the canopy of the team truck in the paddock. Beers and wine flowing freely, more celebrations again, life is good!

Because the race in Holland is on Saturday, practice began on Thursday morning, with qualifying the following day, Friday.

Allan did not qualify well in 31st position, but recovered in the race somewhat, to finish 14th. He doesn't enjoy the circuit in Assen, and it showed.

The team headed back to Barcelona. They would not attend the next race in Belgium, although Alberto would once again fly in to the event.

The paddock in Spa-Francorchamps is terraced in several levels. Naturally the factory teams are placed on the lowest level. The rest of the teams are staggered in various locations up the hill according to their status, which IRTA pre-determined.

We were quite used to being told where to set up, and once you were placed, that was it for the weekend, except this particular weekend!

As usual it was raining cats and dogs. The Ardenne region of Belgium is notorious for wet weather.

This was good for Allan Scott however. He was a rain specialist and he would benefit from a wet race.

Back in the paddock we had set everything up and had begun to set up the bikes, the usual stuff, go to Dunlop for tires, talk to HRC about settings and that sort of thing.

Quite unexpectedly, Mike Trimby, the number one man at IRTA, came into our little compound and told us we would have to move to a higher level. He was, I believe, truly sorry to do this, but he had been told by Mr. Ecclestone that the TV cameras were catching sight of what he called "The Gypsies", and they had to go!

"We had heard that Bernie Ecclestone was becoming involved with bike racing, and that it would likely mean good things were about to happen for the bike racing world......."

We had heard that Bernie Ecclestone was becoming involved with bike racing, and that it would likely

Bernie Ecclestone sent an apologetic Mike Trimby to remove us "Gypsies" from the view of the TV audience.

mean good things were about to happen for the bike racing world. After all, Bernie had been a struggling rider back in the early days of his meteoric career, Everyone knew this about him, and assumed he would be simpatico towards the bike fraternity!

It was hard to swallow, but we broke camp and moved up the hill!

We had barely repositioned, when we were told that it still was possible for the cameras to see us "Gypsy's", and we must move again. So much for thinking Bernie was one of us!

Allan was riding well in practice and qualified 14th. In the race he was literally stalking Ezio Gianola and Hans Spaan, the 1st and 2nd place riders, biding his time before he would take over the lead.

It was not to be. The gear shift linkage broke and he was forced to retire. This was probably his most memorable race, and could have been a turning point in his career. A win at Spa would have been tremendous.

Alberto was equally shaken by Allan's bad luck, but the boss in the Canary Islands was thrilled by this near miss. There would be more great performances to come from Allan.

The rain never let up the whole weekend, and at one point during the night, I was awakened by the sight and sound of a veritable stream rushing through the tent I was sharing with Rolf Korrmann.

Broken gear shift linkage and a dejected father and son.

Our camp beds were only inches off the asphalt,

and I remember looking over to him and laughing, I could reach out and touch the deluge as it raced past. Still we never got wet, tucked away in our snug sleeping bags. Never a dull moment in Belgium, and I was also suffering a terrible hangover from too many Stella Artois. What ever you do, watch out for the Stella!

Overnight, most of the teams had pulled out and headed for Le Mans, France, so the paddock was deserted when I got up in the morning. Trevor Manley was still here, over on the far side of this level.

Nobody was in any rush to pack up, so we had breakfast and looked at our route to France on our well worn Michelin guide. This was long before GPS folks!

We heard Trevor calling us over to his little caravan. When we got there, we were astonished to see a telephone sitting right in the center of his small dining table. I asked him where he got the phone, and was it working?

Apparently it was operational. IRTA had packed up their mobile office and left the phone for collection by the Belgian phone company. The wily Trevor got to it first, while foraging during the night, as he often did.

You can guess what happened next. People were lined up and placing calls all over the planet. Trevor was having a great time giving free phone service to all and Sundry. When we arrived at Le Mans, it was common knowledge that IRTA's phone had been compromised. It had to be the damned Aussies!

IRTA knew who did it initially, and when we were being placed in the paddock, Jacque, the French paddock marshal, winked and said, I have placed you and the Australians close to the telephone junction box, just to make it easy for you, and he winked again with a big smile.

Of course there was a huge hue and cry, that dogged all of us throughout the rest of the season. I told Allan and Jeff to stay out of this mess, and at all cost, do not admit to anything or make deals to confess. Allan Scott Racing was a paid contract team now. We could not afford to become embroiled in a scandal!

Even when we were back home in Pleasant Hill at the end of the season, we were still getting calls from the Belgian phone company.

"..........I learned a lot about the resilience and resourcefulness of Australians. if I were stranded in some impossible place, I would want to be with the Aussies for sure!"

Darren Milner was another Australian rider, who was traveling with his wife Carol. I doubt that he was one of the Aussie night raiding parties, but we were all lumped together now, in the paddock these days. I learned a lot about the resilience and resourcefulness of Australians. if I were stranded in some impossible place, I would want to be with the Aussies for sure!

I had become quite friendly with another group of Australians, the mother and stepfather of Mick Doohan.

Mick was a factory Honda rider, well on his way to many World Championship titles. His motorhome was driven and cared for by his parents, and his step-dad was a Scottish emigrant like me, who had chosen Australia for his new life.

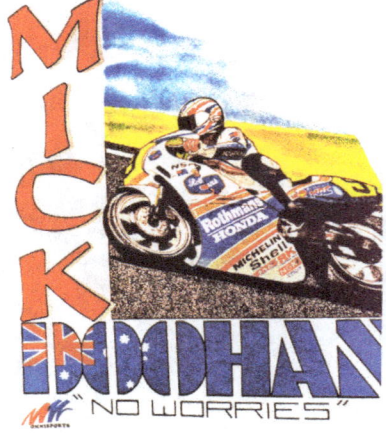

This T-shirt artwork, along with that of many of the top riders of the era, was penned by Allan's older brother David G. Scott.

Mick's mom was a jewel. She would come over to our spot in the Paddock and bring a bunch of Mick's used knee scrapers. Factory guys had to be immaculate when performing, not a single scratch on any equipment was allowed.

Doohan also from time to time, would buy sets of tires for Milner and Manley. I always enjoyed visiting the Doohan camp.

Sadly, Trevor Manley would be in serious trouble at the British Grand Prix, where his season would come to an end, more about this later.

Allan qualified extremely well in 12th place, and was up with the leaders, only to suffer a piston seizure with just four laps to go!

We were now headed for our home grand prix, The British at Donington Park, England. Although we lived in California, we were Scottish born and had a big following in the UK, plus we were all eager to see our family members again. They were coming over from San Francisco to join us, and The Tartan Army were coming south from Scotland as well!

When we got to Calais for the ferry crossing to Dover I warned Jeff, who had a US passport, to say as little as possible when questioned by the British customs and Immigration guys, especially when asked what he was doing in the UK.

Allan had a British passport, I had both a British and a US passport, so naturally we breezed through the process. Jeff however, blew it when he told them he was a tourist basically, but was working for Allan, helping him with his racing career. That did it!

Step out of the truck Mr. Markus, said the customs officer, you need a work permit to enter the UK, follow me!

Two hours later, and after a whole lot of pleading by me, they allowed him into the country. Jeff asked me how I managed to spring him, and I told him that I explained that he (Jeff) was a dreamer and an old school chum of Allan's, who was never allowed near the bikes because he was a blithering idiot, with no mechanical skills whatsoever, just a tourist along for the thrill of the racing!

Happily it was just the 17th of July. We had until August 4th until we would need to be at Donington for practice and qualifying, so off we went to Scotland for some home cooking and haggis!

Akimoto of JHA in Japan told us that he was coming to the British Grand Prix, and would be bringing some new parts and a technician. This was great news for Allan and the team.

Sure enough, "Aki" showed up with a mechanic and a young Japanese lady, who could speak a reasonable amount of English. It helped a great deal.

However, she thought that my wife and sister-in-law, were staff members, and would regularly pop her head into the Mercedes truck, with an order for 'Two tea and one coffee please" for Aki san and the tech?"

I asked Jean to go along with this. We all thought it was hilarious that the girl had assumed that Jean and Elspeth were servants!

Alberto Xiol of Coronas was also present and did

Scotty with Alberto of Coronas and the Japanese translator from JHA at the British G.P.

The Coronas logo had been changed to "Canarias" because of the tobacco ban in Brittain. David, David Jr. Alberto and Akimoto back Allan prior to the British Grand Prix.

not feel comfortable with the JHA team working on the bikes, but I calmed him down by explaining that they had come all the way from Japan with some special parts, and everything was at their expense. What could be wrong with that deal?

"Allan was flying in practice. The JHA parts had had a noticeable effect. An astonishingly quick last lap in qualifying placed him in 5th place and a front row spot on the grid.... Wow!"

Allan was flying in practice. The JHA parts had had a noticeable effect. An astonishingly quick last lap in qualifying placed him in 5th place and a front row spot on the grid....Wow!

Over in the Trevor Manley team, things were going terribly wrong.

Right in the middle of qualifying, Trevor had been arrested as the result of a sting operation by the British plain clothes police and IRTA. They had unearthed a sizeable amount of counterfeit Paddock passes in Trevor's caravan, and had marched him off to jail in nearby Derby.

A wave of panic swept through the whole Paddock. How many people had bought these passes from Trevor, and how many folks had simply gone to a Canon color copy machine and printed their own fake pass?

IRTA had incorporated a hologram on credentials this season, but it was difficult to spot the difference between a fake and the real thing, unless you inspected it closely. Most gate personnel never had time to check them.

Everybody was doing this, in one form or another. Trevor, unfortunately went in to mass production!

Back at the organizers notice board, the time sheets showed that Allan would start alongside Dutchman Hans Spaan, Spaniard Jorge Martinez, Italian Ezio Gianola and Spaniard Alex Criville, all of whom were factory riders on priceless motorcycles! Bravo privateer Allan Scott.

Because of the tobacco advertising ban in the UK, the likes of Marlboro and Cornoas had to cover up signage on trucks, bikes and leathers. We became the Canarias team, Spanish for Canaries, which was of course the island H.Q of our sponsor.

It is almost impossible to express how delighted everyone on the team felt. The Japanese were happy, the Spanish were happy and the Tartan Army were singing over their pints at the Redgate Bar well into the night.

The British circuit announcers were also raving that there had not been a British front row qualifier in the 125 class EVER, to their knowledge, even though Allan was now known as the "Scottish born Californian of Mediterranean descent", on this day he was a full blown Brit!

Unfortunately he would only complete 16 laps of the race, the battle for the podium was fierce. Hans Spaan had pulled out a one second advantage from the lead group, and would not be caught, Allan's pace was equal to the others in contention, but the bike started to fade, he cruised in to the paddock, before something catastrophic, and expensive took place in the engine. Game over for us at Donington Park!

Still in all, there was jubilation in our camp that day, what a performance on a privateer bike, Yikes!

Once again everyone went their separate ways, the Tartan Army back up north, Jean and son David to S.F, Alberto to Barcelona and the Japanese back to Tokyo….wrong!

Aki said that they were coming to Sweden as well, and would simply follow us in the rental car.

I had bad news for him. The ferry from Harwich had to be reserved months in advance. It was very unlikely that they would get on this boat.

After a short group discussion in Japanese, Aki told me that he would follow us to Harwich anyway, and take a chance on a cancellation!

I knew this was a very long shot indeed, and I got out the maps and showed him the alternative route via Dover and through several countries, ferries and many road miles, to get to Anderstorp in Sweden. He looked pensive.

We all watched from the upper deck of our ferry, as predicted, they did not get aboard, and we watched them turn around and head out of the terminal. I was quite sure we had seen the last of Aki and his small crew, and I felt really sorry for them.

"Arriving at the circuit a couple of days later, we were stunned and overjoyed to see Aki and his two colleagues waiting for us………."

Arriving at the circuit a couple of days later, we were stunned and overjoyed to see Aki and his two colleagues waiting for us. They had made the epic journey by land and sea, and arrived slightly ahead of us......Now that is dedication!

IRTA was still trying to pin down the culprits who hijacked the phone in Belgium. I told Neil Bird of IRTA to get to hell out of my face or else. We had a race to run.

The weather was perfect, and Allan was still on his Donington form, qualifying 5th, and securing a front row start once again.

In the race, Allan was once again engaged in a dog fight for the podium, eventually clinching 7th place. It was a nerve racking race to watch and I was glad when it ended. For some reason I felt that this would not be a good place to get injured. It just seemed to be so far away from central Europe.

We wished Aki and his two team members Bon Voyage, as they left on the return journey to London, and finally home to Tokyo.

Front row in Sweden: Alex Criville, Hans Spaan, Jorge Martinez, Allan Scott.

Jeff, Scotty, Joan Joanoff JHA Lady and Allan.

They were very satisfied with the performance of Allan, and they left Jeff with a number of special parts to finish out the Grand Prix season in Czechoslovakia.

The Czech people were enjoying their new found freedom. It was a changed place compared to the year before, and it was good to be back under these conditions, although the cost of living was noticeably higher now.

I probably mentioned previuosly that Allan adored the circuit here at Brno, and had a lot of fans locally, and from East Germany. They wrote to him many times, asking for autographs and photos.

"There were close to 250.000 spectators on race day, and the 125 race was another tough skirmish."

There were close to 250.000 spectators on race day, and the 125 race was another tough skirmish.

Allan qualified in 8th, and was on the second row of the grid, and finished in the same place after a terrific duel with the leading group.

This was the end of the season for most teams and riders, and they would all be heading back to their various homelands. This was not the case for us.

Allan had been approached by Carlo Pernat of Cagiva in Brno. Would he like to test the 500cc Cagiva?

A test session was being set up at Ryjeka in Yuogslavia. The invited riders were Kevin McGee of Australia, British rider Ron Haslam, Alexander Barros of Brasil and Allan Scott, the Scottish born Californian of Mediterranean descent!

"This could very easily be the big break for Allan....."

This could very easily be the big break for Allan. Never mind about the big opportunity. Allan just wanted a shot at that beast, normally ridden by Randy Mamola, who was not sure he would renew his contract for 1990.

A date was set and we headed for Ryjeka. A hotel was reserved for Allan, Jeff and I, and we met Carlo Pernat, George Vukmanovitch and the team to go over the ground rules for the test.

Each rider would do one day of testing. No other rider would be allowed to observe. The rider's manager would provide Carlo with a proposal/contract if possible at the end of the test.

I would have to borrow a typewriter at the hotel, and come up with numbers. I had no idea what would work for Cagiva. I only knew that it would be a whole lot more money than the Coronas contract.

The test was going well, and Allan was slowly improving each lap he completed. In the middle of the day Alex Barros appeared uninvited and

A Gagiva mechanic and Jeff look on as Allan prepares to test the 500cc Cagiva in Yuogalavia.

wouldn't leave. He was not supposed to be there and I think it put Allan off his stride a little, maybe yes, maybe no.

I met with Carlo in the evening and presented my proposal. He was an easy guy to get along with, and he said he would give it his utmost attention.

A decision would depend on Randy Mamola renewing his contract or not. If he did not, it would mean an American would likely be signed to replace him. This is pure logic in marketing for Cagiva.

Randy did renew his deal. Alex Barros got the second contract because of his effectiveness for the Brazilian market that was as yet untapped by Cagiva,

Allan had been so close to joining the premier class.

We made our way back to London to prepare for our return home to California.

When we reached Wallington, our UK base, there was a message from Dennis Noyes, a journalist with the Spanish magazine SoloMoto. Can Allan compete in the Annual Superprestigio in Calafat on September 24th?

"This was a great honor, to be selected by the organizers by virtue of your performance during the past season, was high tribute indeed."

This was a great honor, to be selected by the organizers by virtue of your performance during the past season, was high tribute indeed.

We agreed on the expenses fee, and decided to leave a bike with the Coronas team in Martorell, Spain. They would meet us at the circuit on the weekend of the race. They warned us that they had no racing fuel and asked us for help with this.

Allan (#10) tails Ezio Gianola and Alex Criville in the Annual Superprestigio in Calafat Spain.

With three weeks until the Superprestigio, Allan and Jeff wanted to go home, so that was what we did.

In the meantime, I was arranging for a barrel of 115 octane US racing fuel to be shipped to the Coronas team, for collection at Barcelona airport.

Repsol, the giant Spanish oil company, lodged a protest with Customs at the airport. It was hours before it was released, and only when I accused Repsol of rigging the eventual result of the race this weekend in Calafat.

As no racing fuel was available in Spain to riders without a Repsol contract, it was obvious that we had to bring fuel with us to Calafat. I guaranteed the Customs guys that I would raise a major stink if my rider was excluded because Repsol said so, and I would demand sizeable compensation, most of all I would tell the world of motorcycle sport just how corrupt the Spanish authorities and the sport were. That did it!

Pepe and I finally got clearance to collect the fuel on the Saturday of the morning practice. There was a lot of nail biting until we got back from Barcelona airport. Nothing comes easy in this business.

The race took the usual form, Allan mixing it up

with Alex Criville, Ezio Gianola and Jorge Martinez, only to have the power fade in the last few laps as he fell back to 7th place....Now the season was really over at last!........No it was not quite done yet. When I called Jean at home in California to give her the results, she told me there had been a call from Japan. Would I call this number in Japan and ask for Ko Gotoh.

He wanted to discuss the possibility of Allan testing one of his 250cc Yamaha's at an upcoming race in Tsukuba, Japan.

He was a Yamaha factory supported team owner, competing in the All Nippon National series. Allan had been recommended to him by Terry Griffen, a friend with a business in Berkeley, California, who knew Ko Gotoh. He had put Allan forward as a prime candidate.

Ko's company would pay all expenses if we agreed to come. I said I would let him know when I returned to San Francisco in a few days.

We returned to Martorell and began to pack up our gear. Everything went fine until we realized we still had a moped to deal with, shucks!

There were always young kids hanging around the race shop, so when Joan Jornet said he had no use for the little Honda Express moped, we simply gave it to one of the kids. That started a big possession fight amongst them, and they were still battling when we left for the shipper in Barcelona.

Allan and Jeff went with Pepe and our gear, and I went to Alberto's office in Barcelona to close out our contract, We were flying to London later in the day, and I wanted to put this behind us.

All the numbers added up fine, so Alberto called his secretary to make a cheque out for the agreed amount. I said that I did not want a cheque, only cash would work.

We had been working on a cash basis all along, so I felt that it was not an unreasonable request, although it was quite a fair amount of Ptas.

"…..he felt that we would have a tough time getting out of Spain with the cash."

Pepe and the boys were back now, and Alberto assigned Pepe to go to the bank and cash the cheque for us. Pepe was not happy. Alberto wasn't either because he felt that we would have a tough time getting out of Spain with the cash. He may well be right I said, we would soon find out!

On the way to the airport in Barcelona, I divided up the cash into three equal packages, one for Allan, one for Jeff and one for me. I was really worried about Jeff. Would he repeat what he did in Dover?....and I warned him to keep his mouth shut.

The security check point looked formidable, with armed guards posted all around. I knew there was a limit to how much cash could be taken out of Spain. We would really be in big trouble if we were searched.

As soon as we started to place all of our carry-on baggage on the conveyor belt, helmets, leathers, gloves and the like, the security guys started yelling Spanish, then grabbed Allan and started shaking his hand and slapping him on the back. They knew him from watching the Grand Prix's on television, and had watched the Superprestigio at the weekend. They called all the guards over and Allan began signing autographs. In the mean time they cleared all of our baggage!

I had risked all, and dodged yet another bullet!

We still had to come through Heathrow in London, and San Francisco in California. Would our luck hold, would we make it home with our legitimate contract cash earnings. Fortunately we did.

Back home in Pleasant Hill, California, I contacted Ko Gotoh in Tokyo once more, and told him that Allan, Jeff and I would come for the test.

He said that we would be met at Narita by someone from Yamaha, and be taken to the hotel in downtown Tokyo. The following day we would go to his office to discuss the deal he had in mind.

That first evening we were brought to a restaurant for dinner. I was blown away by the appearance of Terry Griffen and his pregnant wife. They were also guests of Ko Gotoh tonight.

I never asked if the Griffens had come over at their own expense or Ko Gotoh's, but I sure was surprised to see them.

I had been told by Terry that Ko owned a lot of department stores in Japan and was very wealthy.

He also told me that Ko had been educated at UC Berkeley, and was a pretty decent race car driver, and had raced at Sears Point, my local circuit in Northern California. It's a small, small world.

Ko finally showed up and joined the group. He introduced himself to us and said that tonight was for relaxing and pleasure. He welcomed everyone to Japan. Tomorrow we would speak about the test and the deal he had in mind.

"He spoke perfect English, a noticeably polished man who exuded confidence and control. I liked him right away."

He spoke perfect English, a noticeably polished man who exuded confidence and control. I liked him right away.

A driver picked us up at the Shibuya Tokyu Inn and delivered us to a big department store. This was Ko Gotoh's business office, in fact it was one of his many such stores in Japan.

He described his plan for Allan. His Yamaha 250cc team wanted a fresh from Europe, seasoned World ranked rider, to ride for them in the All Nippon Championship series in 1990.

Allan could have Jeff along with him. They would have an apartment, food, utilities and a Toyota mini-van.

He could keep any personal sponsor income, such as helmet contracts and all prize money.

They would be given one round trip ticket each to San Francisco during the year. As Allan's manager, I would also be given one round trip ticket. Doe's it sound pretty good?

No contract fee would be offered for Allan Scott Racing's services. This was not what I had in mind, and told him so right away.

He wasn't fazed by my reaction, or appeared not to be. He said I should talk it over tonight. In the mean time he had set up a tour of Tokyo for us, and a visit to the racing offices later that day.

There were two companies representing Ko's racing team. The Clipping Point Corporation, whose business card read…"The Sales of Sense and System Promotion".

The second company was the Cheetah Corporation, which I knew to be the technical side of the team. In essence the bikes were prepared by Cheetah.

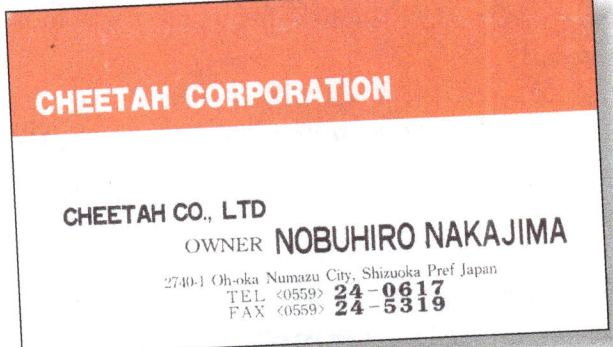

While we were at Clipping Point's offices, we bumped into Roberto Gallina, the Italian owner of Team Gallina, and the sponsor of the Italian rider, Pier Francisco Chili, the number 6 rated rider in the 500cc class.

He knew the Ko Gotoh, Clipping Point/Cheetah operation, so I asked him a few questions about their deal offer, which I told him at once was likely to be a no go for us.

I told him something he already knew, that Allan was a rider who was number 10 in the 125 World standings. Why would I bring him out of Europe, when he was on the brink of a factory ride in 1990 and he had been assured by HRC that he would get the Honda RS125 'A' kit for his assault on the 1990 championship? (see later).

Roberto listened to me. He had his own problems, trying to convince Honda to let him lease two 500's for 1990. I believe he did get bikes, but they were not to the standard he had requested, and PFC slipped back to 11th in the World in 1990.

How much did I want for Allan to move to Japan for the All Nippon Series? I told him the number I had in mind, and he laughed. "Dave, they don't have that kind of money to spend", he said.

We moved the next day to the town of Tsukuba, where the circuit was located. It was in an area of beautiful Japanese farmland, the fields being actively worked by folk in straw sun hats. The scene was spectacular to me. It reminded me of a scene from The Seven Samurai.

In Tsukuba we met Mrs. Gotoh for the first time. She was to be the liaison between us and Ko. She seemed quite young and very bright, and she also spoke perfect English, for which I was most grateful!

Ko joined us for one more dinner, this time with the full team in attendance, managers, riders and technicians.

"I was about to make one of my fatal mistakes this evening".

I was about to make one of my fatal mistakes this evening.

After the meal, everyone followed Ko into the adjoining bar and pool room. Would anyone care to play a game with me, asked Ko?

I was a decent pool player, so I said I would play him, and we set up the table with the whole team watching.

Ko was quite good too, but I couldn't resist taking on the challenge and easily beat him. The atmosphere became quite gloomy all of a sudden. I had beaten the boss. This was the clear signal I was receiving, and I knew at that moment, that I should have yielded the game to him. That event was the first of several errors I made in Japan. Lost in translation I called it!

This was when I could have used the wisdom of my close friend David Fender, a 30-plus year executive with American Honda in California. He is a Welshman, a Celt like me, but very skilled in Japanese culture, and he did coach me on Japanese protocol from time to time. I would in fact fax him during this trip, when I ran into problems with HRC. I also told him I was having a tough time over here in Japan, and wished he were here to bail me out!

Prior to agreeing to the test with Yamaha, I had faxed HRC and asked if there would be any problem or conflict if Allan did this test. The reply was……"no problem, good luck, see you at Tsukuba. (see later)

We first laid eyes on the bikes in the garage, which actually was a part of the Yamaha factory team in Tsukuba. Two very nicely prepared models for the Japanese team riders, and another one sitting a little farther away, looking anything but ready to race. The number 06 was on it. I assumed that this was the one Allan was to ride.

I asked Ko's wife if this was the bike for Allan. She relied that it was, and I blew a fuse! (this was my second mistake of the trip).

Staff members of Team Itoen. •. Allan and three of the team riders.

I told her that the team had to clearly understand that Allan was a total racer, and it was my responsibility to make sure that he had perfect equipment when he went out onto the race track. The 06 bike was a disgrace, and I wanted it brought up to the same standard as the other two machines. She said she would speak to her husband in Tokyo, and get back to me.

The team technicians had picked up on my concern, and were hurriedly making adjustments and stuff to the 06 bike. I looked it over and told Allan to go out, but to be very careful for the first few laps.

He fell off the bike after just a couple of laps, fortunately with no real damage to rider or bike.

Mrs. Gotoh told me that she had told her husband that I was upset about the lack of preparation on the 06 Allan Scott bike.

He told her to let me know that he was coming to the race tomorrow by helicopter. If I felt uncomfortable with the bike, don't let Allan race tomorrow.

"I was speechless. How could we have come all this way to Japan, and not actually race?"

I was speechless. How could we have come all this way to Japan, and not actually race?

How could I tell Allan that it made no difference, he was raring to go, and would insist on racing tomorrow. (I think this episode was another one of my mistakes).

Race day dawned, and Allan had qualified on the back row of the grid. Ko Gotoh was now at the circuit, and asked me to join him for tea and talks.

I reiterated my concern for the poor preparation on number 06. He absolutely blew me away, when he told me that they had already accepted Allan as their rider, and never intended him to actually ride at Tsukuba. They just wanted to make the deal, and did not need any test ride. They simply wanted to get to know him better. How do you figure that?

Allan didn't know about this conversation, and rode a safe race running in 17th with Thomas Stevens, the Lucky Strike Team Roberts rider. On the 8th lap, a piston broke on the 06 bike, and Allan was forced to retire.

As a matter of interest, in a field of 32 riders, there were only three non Japanese, Thomas Stevens, USA, Darryl Beattie, Australia and Allan Scott, Scottish born Californian of Mediterranean descent!

We returned to the Shibuya Tokyu Inn in Tokyo. The next evening was to be the final meeting with Ko. He would reimburse us for air fares and any other expenses at that time, and he would also give us his decision, whether he was interested in negotiating further.

He arrived on time and paid me the expenses in American Express Travelers cheques. He did not want to negotiate any more, (nor did I) and he wished us a safe journey home.

I thanked him, and asked what time our ride to the airport would arrive tomorrow morning. He smiled and said.."Take the bus to the airport" and walked out of the hotel.

I looked at Allan and Jeff in amazement. We better find out how we get this airport bus fellas, the party was over".

The concierge rang my room and said I had a fax at the front desk.

It was from Honda HRC telling me that they would not now support Allan Scott Racing in 1990, and that it had absolutely nothing to do with him riding a factory Yamaha at Tsukuba……..**Oh yeah?**

In the morning at breakfast we had figured out how to get to Narita airport for our flight back to California, when we saw one of the team riders coming towards us, smiling and handing us chocolates. He indicated that he was here to take Scott san to the airport. Ko Gotoh did not send him he said, he had come on his own out of respect for Allan, a fellow racer.

When I was checking out our group at the front desk, the clerk showed me a bill for our stay. I told him that the cost was to be charged to Ko Gotoh of Team Itoen. After all, was he not the owner of this hotel as well?

This young Japanese rider took it upon himself to come to our hotel and take us to the airport.

The young Japanese rider spoke no English, but he, Allan and Jeff seemed to get along just fine, and chattered all the way to Narita, proving to me that motorcycle racers do indeed share a common language.

As the 747 climbed out of Narita, I was taking stock of this incredible week in Japan. The final touch to an amazing year. Nobody would believe this fantastic 1989 season, which I was now sure had finally come to an end. I wondered and began mentally planning for 1990.

I have to mention in closing this story, that there was an unforgettable event at Tsukba. Not everything was negative.

Hiroshi Hasegawa

I got to meet **Hiroshi Hasegawa**, a veteran Yamaha development rider, who actually raced in the Isle of Man TT in 1963.

He was one of Yamaha's most respected retired riders, and would be honored forever by the factory.

There he was, shooting the breeze about the old days with Yamaha. I was introduced by Ko Gotoh, and I sat down beside him.

I told him that I knew who he was. He was stunned and said, "You do?".

I told him that I did not remember the year he came to Europe, but mentioned that I did know that he was the main rider responsible for the development of the Yamaha TD series race bikes, TD1A, TD1B and the model I had raced in California, the TD1C. These bikes were to revolutionize privateer racing all over the world.

Fumio Ito was his team mate in 1963. Fumio came to California in the same year I did, 1967, and I would race against him several times. He was a pleasure to ride with, and he paid me the same compliment.

Hiroshi told me about the awful early days, when he was thrown down the road on a daily basis, by seizures and the like, until the engineers finally figured out how to stop the chrome from peeling off the alloy cylinder walls.

I said I was proud to have met him after all these years.

His card and picture are still in my desk to this day.

GARELLI 1990
The Last Factory Rider

This is a story that I feel has to be told, for reasons known only to Daniele Agrati the owner of Garelli Corse, the year 1990 and the name of the last factory rider, Allan Scott, has been omitted from almost all historic records commissioned by Daniele.

There is apparently a recent publication written by Roberto Patrignani, the Press liaison for Garelli back in1990, a very nice and helpful fellow, who I had the pleasure of meeting again a couple of years ago at the Isle of Man TT races.

He told me that there was a new book which sadly still does not mention or contain any photos of the year with Allan Scott, the book I presently own entitled "Agrati Garelli, 80 anni di storia", written by Daniele Agrati and Roberto Patrignani in 1999, makes a brief mention of the last season 1990 on page 170, but no where in this book are there any photos of Allan Scott.

I have not seen this publication, but I am surprised by Daniele's decision to alter history, I intend to write the real story of Garelli's fall from World Championship fame and the misery felt by everyone involved during that awful final season.

The story really began in November 1989, Allan had done exceptionally well that year and would

Allan sits astride his Garelli at the Dutch TT. American mechanic Jeff Marcus holds the shade-bearing umbrella while one of the factory mechanics stands to Allan's left.

be ranked number 10 in 1989. He was among the top privateers now and being scouted by several teams.

I was on top of the world as his manager/partner/promoter/father and it was quite clear to me that his talent was limited only by the machinery

The author David Scott with Daniele Agrati (right) and Garelli Press Liaison Roberto Patrignani, shown at the Isle of Man vintage event. Dave Fender photo

we could afford, which amounted to a pair of box stock Honda RS125's.

Every two years in Milan, there is a gigantic motorcycle and bicycle Expo at the location called the Fiera, and I decided to go there with a view to buying or leasing an ex-factory bike. Leasing was growing in popularity as a means of acquiring very expensive race bikes, I had to find out if it was a feasible option for us at Allan Scott Racing.

We had two new Honda's on order for 1990, but it was still only November 1989 and there was lots of time to speculate, plus it was the best place in the world to campaign for sponsors and to mingle with the movers and shakers of the sport, and of course meet with our friends the riders who would be there on the same mission perhaps.

I arranged credentials and flew into Malpensa, the international airport outside of Milan, I had made no hotel arrangements and took the airporter bus into the center of Milan at the main railway station, figuring that it shouldn't be a big deal to find a room for the night.

That particular part of Milan is the hunting ground of gypsy folk, young and old, begging for money and picking pockets of unsuspecting tourists, especially Americans who carry wallets in the back pocket of their pants, I actually saw a small boy take the wallet off a guy who was bent over reaching for his luggage in the cargo well of the bus, the kid was gone in a flash.

I was carrying $7.000.00 cash which I felt could be used as a sign of serious intent should I be lucky enough to make a deal, if those gypsies surrounding me had only known how much I was worth, I may never have gotten out of Milan alive!

My room for the night was in a really sleezy building just off the main railway plaza, I am sure it was the haunt of the worst creatures of the night for the check-in window was wire mesh and you had to slip the cash(lira) through a very small slot and when accepted, a room key came through from a suspicious check in clerk.

I was thrashed from the long flight to Italy and showered before bed, I stuffed the cash under my pillow and was asleep in seconds.

My route next morning to the Fiera was simple and I headed out first thing after turning in my key, although I had no intention of coming back, I told the hotel that I might stay another night.

The Fiera is reached by underground and I was soon on a train with the morning commuters, two stations into the journey I almost had a heart attack!

I had left the $7.000.00 under the pillow in the flea-bag hotel. I thought I was going to collapse but managed to get off the train and doubled back to the hotel.

Feeling that the room may have already be cleaned and the bed made up, I was convinced that the money would be gone and the people who ran the hotel would no doubt deny any knowledge of my cash.

I nervously went to the wire mesh window and asked if I could get the room key back for a moment. The woman could not speak English, but she agreed eventually to let me have it. All the time I could hear the sound of the maid vacuuming and going from room to room cleaning.

Opening that room door was one of the most daunting events of my life. The bed looked made up. The maid had obviously been in this room.

"I had just dodged a mighty big bullet......"

I reached under the pillow and could not believe that the cash was still there. Could the maid have just straightened the bed, failing to lift the pillows?.......who cares!...... I had just dodged a mighty big bullet and I got out of there as fast as my feet could carry me!

Back on the subway to the Fiera, I was gathering my thoughts and thinking to myself just how lucky could I get?

Inside the Expo, I soon met up with lots of riders and industry people, and I let everyone know why I was here. Most thought I was nuts to try and secure an ex-factory machine, but I pressed on anyway.

I spoke with all of the leading manufacturers including Garelli, who had a very nice stand staffed by really friendly people, who also thought I was nuts to even think I could buy a sacred Garelli, but told me that Daniele Agrati was the boss (I already knew this) and that he would be on the stand later in the day.

When I finally sat down with Daniele, he told me to call him Dani. I found him to be charming, educated and a true enthusiast of the G.P scene, without a doubt very proud of the achievements of Garelli Corse over the years. I too respected their many championship results and World titles, but I also knew that they were having a difficult time with the new single cylinder formula in the 125cc class.

They had dominated the twin cylinder class for many years, but the transition to singles was not immediately successful and they were struggling for answers. I also knew that Jan Thiel was the engineer and that it was a fair bet he would solve the lack-lustre performance of the Garelli 125. Sadly it never improved much in the year ahead, 1989.

Nevertheless, I got on well with Dani and asked him to keep Allan Scott in mind for the future.

As a matter of interest, the following statistics show how Garelli fared in 1989:

- Spanish Grand Prix - No entry
- Italian Grand Prix - 13th Domenico Brigaglia
- German Grand Prix - 17th Domenico Brigaglia
- Austrian Grand Prix - 7th Domenico Brigaglia
- Dutch T.T. - 16th Domenico Brigaglia
- Belgian Grand Prix - 11th Domenico Brigaglia
- French Grand Prix - 7th Domenico Brigaglia
- British Grand Prix - 6th Domenico Brigaglia
- Swedish T.T. - 22nd Emilo Cuppini
- Czechoslovak Grand Prix - 21st Emilio Cuppini

In contrast to Garelli's troubled year, Allan Scott completed 1989 in 10th overall aboard a standard Honda RS125R.

This is the 125cc Garelli that had won the world championship in 1987 on display at the Milan show.

In the winter of 1989, I had a call from Dani Agrati asking me what Allan's plans were for the coming 1990 season.

During 1989 Allan had been supported technically by JHA a Japanese development company, and sponsored financially by Coronas, a Spanish cigarette company based in the Canary Islands, neither of whom were going to continue with Allan into 1990. I was now open to discuss any possible link with a sponsor or a full contract ride for Allan in the coming year 1990.

Allan in fact started the 1990 season at the Japanese Grand Prix at Suzuka in March, without any commitment to a sponsor for 1990.

The new Honda 125's were always delivered to customers in plain white and fitted with regular spoked wheels, so we had to fit a pair of Marvic magnesium alloys by race time.

I had ordered these from Marvic in Italy, months before in anticipation of Suzuka, but they had not yet arrived in Japan.

After several frantic calls to Alessandro Vicario at the factory in Brunello, Italy, he called me back via the Race Office at the circuit and assured me that the wheels were on board an ALITALIA flight from Milan to Osaka.

It was now Wednesday of race week, so I decided that I would go to Osaka and get the wheels first thing in the morning.

There was apprehension all around that I was about to undertake this fairly long and complex journey, but I was sure it would be a piece of cake and set off at the crack of dawn clutching the flight number and invoice data for the Japanese customs people.

Outside the Suzuka circuit I hopped into a taxi and rode to the Shiroko train station and bought a round trip ticket to Osaka.

My first destination was Nagoya, about 40 minutes away. I then changed trains to get to Osaka, passing through Kyoto, arriving 50 minutes later.

By asking one or two, or maybe it was three or four, of the multitude of Japanese pedestrians, I found a bus to take me to Itami Airport on the north side of Osaka. I was on foot of course and searching for International freight and Customs offices.

I finally located the Customs people who looked really stern, as Japanese men in authority tend to look, but I had learned that this did not always mean that they were mean spirited, in fact we were all joking and laughing within minutes, when they found out that this round eye idiot had come all the way from Suzuka in search of two wheels from Italy!

The head man in the Customs office jokingly asked me why he should help us by releasing these wheels, only to have Allan Scott go out and perhaps beat the local Japanese ace riders? He nevertheless waived the duty and gave me the two large boxes.

Now my problem was how to get these two approximately 3X3X2 foot square boxes back to Suzuka by the way I had gotten here. They were not really heavy, just bulky!

I asked the onlooking and curious Customs guys if they could find me some light rope, which they did quite quickly. They were staring in amazement as I fashioned a method of carrying this load on my own.

It is best described as Chinese Cooly fashion. Two boxes tightly tied with a loop of rope across my shoulders connecting them, each box tucked up under my armpits. What else could I do?

The Customs people waved me off in disbelief as I trotted away to begin the return journey to Suzuka. I made it through the most busy commute time in Japanese daily life. I will never forget that journey. Hats off to the Japanese people who helped me along the way.

First race of 1990 at Suzuka Japan
Dave Fender photos

It was around 10.30 that evening when I got back to the circuit hotel. Allan and Jeff were really concerned for me, but glad to get the two wheels. Sadly I don't think I ever paid Marvic for those wheels, but Alessandro never harried me about the bill.

"Allan's Honda siezed on the very first lap of the race. Such a shame to travel all that distance to Japan and then fail to finiah the race."

Allan's Honda seized on the very first lap of the race. Such a shame to travel all that distance to Japan and then fail to finish the race.

He and Jeff Marcus, his mechanic, and the two Honda's returned to London with the G.P. entourage, to wait at his U.K. base in Wallington, Surrey for the next race in April at the Spanish Grand Prix in Jerez. I returned to San Francisco.

Dani and Garelli were one of several teams interested in Allan, the main difference being that Garelli was a factory team with a racing budget, the others wanted Allan to buy a ride with them. It wasn't too difficult to give Dani at least a chance to lay out his plan for Garelli and Allan.

It was no secret that all of the seeded Italian riders had no interest in riding a Garelli anymore, and I knew that this would be a very tough ride to take over and follow in the footsteps of the likes of Nieto, Gresini, Lazzarini, Bianchi, Brigaglia, Cadalora, Reyes, Cuppini and many others all of whom had been with Garelli in the glory days of dominance in 50cc and 125cc racing.

Dani also knew that he had a hard sell if he was to put together a deal with the number 10 ranked 125 rider in the world, who had spent the last two years easily blowing past the Garelli riders struggling to even qualify.

It was not going to be easy for me either. Allan had little knowledge of the real history attached to Garelli, but I knew it was a great chance to be a genuine factory rider, and perhaps….just perhaps, he might actually sort this bike out and make it a winner again. If nothing else he was destined to become a part of Garelli history. (I never dreamed he would in fact be denied his rightful place in history as the last Garelli contracted rider.)

So I spoke with Allan and his mechanic Jeff, giving them my opinion and the pros and cons of a potential ride with Garelli….Allan agreed to give it a try-out at the Spanish Grand Prix in April, Jeff would accompany him and if the test ride worked for him, we would go straight back to the factory in Montocello and try to write a contract for the rest of 1990.

I flew to Jerez to join Allan, Jeff and the Garelli team for the preliminary try out. It wasn't very inspiring for Allan who felt that this bike was a long way away from being competitive, but I felt that we ought to go to Monticello anyway and at least talk it over, and if the negotiations failed we would simply head back to London, pick up our two Hondas and get on with the season as privateers.

Dani never realized that I was not hopping back on a plane to San Francisco, but was in fact staying for negotiations and that I expected him to pay for my flight to Milan. He had after all agreed to cover the expense of the test. I was now a part of that expense. He was not at all happy to pay my fare back to Italy.

The flight to Milan was full of riders and team mechanics, and it was easy to read the body language and grins of the guys who thought we were making a huge mistake if we went with Garelli, I doubt that Allan picked up on it though.

"Monticello turned out to be a delightful small town, just the way you see them in the travel brochures…"

Monticello turned out to be a delightful small town, ….Just the way you see them in travel brochures, including the endless church bells. Dani Agrati grew up here and everyone knew him wherever we went.

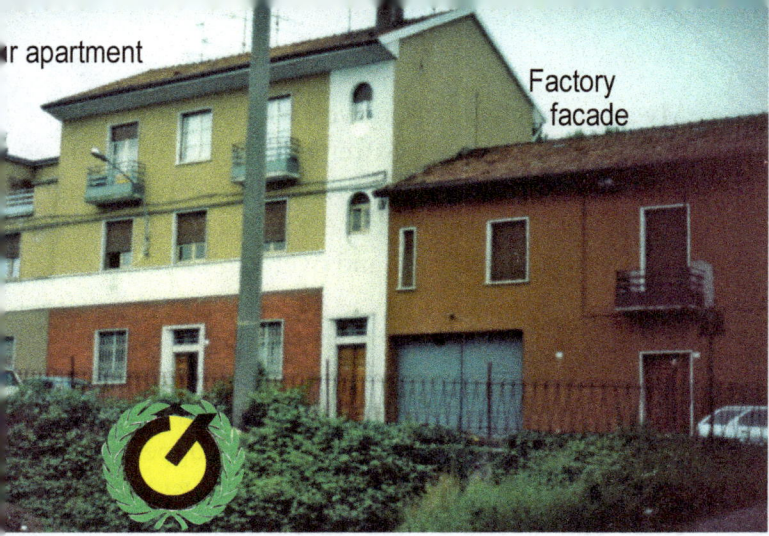
Factory facade

View from apartment balcony

The Garelli factory was a full blown manufacturer, turning out mainly mopeds back in 1990, but you would never know it was there, tastefully designed to blend in with the small Italian township of Monticello, the main office facades in brown sandstone disguised it's very existence by merging in with the neighboring buildings.

Walking into this very special place was a moving experience for me. Many famous riders had come through these doors and I knew the history of this great company.

The board room was a typical old world oak paneled room surrounded by display cases with World Championship trophies and assorted pictures of the past great riders, mainly Italians. I doubt that any group such as we had ever graced this room. I was in awe to say the least.

The factory was abuzz with the news that Allan could possibly be the new rider and we could feel it as we were led on a tour of the plant. A few workers gave us the thumbs-up sign, and others were not so charming, especially those with posters of Fausto Gresini above their workplace.

The race shop was well equipped and had a fully enclosed dyno room. This was Jan Thiel's territory, I knew he was a brilliant Dutch engineer who had had a hand in the design and development of many very successful race engines, including a 50cc bike called a Jamathi back in the 1960's. He worked with Minarelli, Bultaco and of course Garelli, if we were to make a deal at Garelli. It would be important to get along with Jan. Jeff would prove to be an asset in this case. He and Jan hit it off and Jeff would spend many hours with Jan assisting him on projects and in the dyno room, often well into the night.

Jeff would also become the darling of the factory canteen ladies, and they set about feeding him huge portions of pasta every day.

The talks began with the usual theme, how much did Allan feel was fair for his services? Before any serious commitments were made, there was the matter of accommodation between races. Where would we live? What would we drive day to day? Where would we eat?

This is pretty heavy stuff to sort out and Dani was noticeably concerned about the costs involved in all of this. I remember asking him that if cost was that big of an issue, what on earth were we doing here?

He started off by giving us an Alfa Romeo station wagon for daily use….nice. We were in a hotel on arrival in Monticello and I suppose that was how Dani planned to house us, however I found out that Jan Thiel actually lived within the factory grounds, in an apartment and that there was another apartment lying empty. I suggested that we take over the vacant rooms, and Dani happily agreed, I also found out that Jan Thiel ate out every evening at a nice little place in town as part of his contract, but Dani rejected the same programme for us.

After a full day of negotiations with Allan and Dani, we signed a deal for the remainder of season 1990, and moved our gear into the apartment.

Jeff, Allan & Jan Thiel
Dave Fender photos

I flew back to San Francisco to make my peace with Jean, making sure that she had all the details of the deal, and letting her know that I would be returning to Misano with my friend Dave Fender of American Honda. We would meet in Frankfurt and pick up a loaner car from Honda Germany and drive to Italy.

As I mentioned, the next race on the G.P. tour was Misano on May 20th, literally a local event for Garelli, held on the Adriatic coast of Italy. So the boys had a little time to clean up the apartment and do laundry. They also took stock of Monticello and found the places to shop for food and the like.

I talked to Dani about setting Allan and Jeff up with a couple of the little Garelli trail bikes. They were needing to get away from the factory environment, the quiet little town and I suspect probably from me.

That worked out well until Jeff trashed his bike, and Dani withdrew both bikes as a result. He worked me over pretty good too, mostly in Italian, but I got the gist of it!

My guys were not coping well with the rather dull apartment life and the extreme quietness of Monticello by night, and quite frankly I had just about had it with Tom Cruise and the video Top Gun which they played over and over again.

When Dave Fender and I arrived in Misano and checked into the hotel where the team were staying and were re-united with Allan and Jeff, we were literally stunned by the sudden appearance of a little blonde California girl with just a backpack. She spotted us and waved. I knew this girl was from our home town of Pleasant Hill, California, and I guessed as a direct result of the publicity at home about Allan joining Garelli, she had simply decided she would hit her piggy bank, pack her bag and go to Misano via Paris and several train rides. After the initial shock and wild greetings, she told us that she had taken two weeks off from her job and wondered how she could get to the next race in Germany. Would she be able to travel with the team?

"She stopped everyone in their tracks when she walked into that hotel, including Dani Agrali. What could I say. There are some incredibly brave folk in this world and she was one of them."

She stopped everyone in their tracks when she walked into that hotel, including Dani Agrati. What could I say. There are some incredibly brave folk in this world and she was one of them.

On the veranda at our hotel in Misano. Allan in front of Jameesa with Dave Scott to the far right. Dave Fender photo

Jameesa "Ding Bat" walks down pit lane at the Nurburgring with the boys. Dave Fender photo

At this point we did not know that Garelli had decided that they would not be going to Germany with the team.

Dave Fender and I therefore agreed to take her with us to the Nurburgring, and at the end of the event Fender would drop her at Frankfurt airport for her return flight home, an incredible finale to a very bold undertaking by an exceptional young woman. By this time I had christened her "The Ding Bat" for even attempting this trip…….her name was actually Jameesa.

However, in Germany she somehow or another over the course of the weekend was renamed "Dingle Bell", thanks mainly to little Willie Scheidauer and Rolf Korrmann's twisting the translation from English to German, and I think probably because she fell asleep at dinner as a result of too much beer!

I had to get back to Italy and luckily hitched a ride to Milan with George Vukmanovitch of Cagiva. He was Freddie Spencer's mechanic for years and now was head technician at Cagiva, which fielded Randy Mamola.

We had a good time talking about our club days racing in California. He was tuning and I was riding.

At Misano I had walked the paddock and checked out the R.V's, noticing that a few of the Italian riders were set up with modest sized motor homes, capable of sleeping four and diesel powered for economy and reliability.

Myself, Jameesa and Dave Fender.

Incidentally, the Italian Grand Prix at Misano did not go well when Allan failed to qualify.

Having several talks with the motor home riders revealed that they were leasing them from a company near Milan, I knew this would solve everything for us, after races we could stay in the paddock amongst all the other riders and journey on to the next race to meet the Garelli team coming from Monticello, we would be out of Dani's hair and the confines of the factory, and probably wouldn't be back to Monticello until the season wrapped up.

Dani did the math and was economically relieved and agreed, so off we went to shop for a small motor home. We found one in nice condition, powered by a Ford diesel and a 4 speed stick shift. Back in Monticello we loaded up that same day and headed for the Salzburgring, in Austria, we had once again rejoined the Grand Prix traveling circus and everyone was happy!

The Austrian Grand Prix is held in a natural bowl/amphitheater setting which is straight out of the movie

Hero Drent photo

A collision early in the race in Austria separated the fairing from the Garelli, but Allan was able to continue in the G.P. Hero Drent photo

"The Sound of Music", considered by most riders to be a dangerous circuit, especially when wet.

"They get masses of spectators and the atmosphere is fantastic, camping overnight and singing all the time, fuelled by gallons of great beer."

They get masses of spectators and the atmosphere is fantastic, camping overnight and singing all the time, fuelled by gallons of great beer.

A memorable moment when heard for the first time, is the 6.a.m. wake up call coming over the loudspeakers in the paddock...Achtung Fahrerlagr!... Actung Fahrerlager! it booms out! Which simply means Attention in the Paddock, but for just a brief moment you think you may have been drafted into the Austrian army during the night!

The Garelli was really flying in practice and it was great to see how this boosted everyone's morale. Was this going to be the breakthrough we all hoped for?

Dani and Jan were really smiling in anticipation of a good result, it was raining sporadically which meant that Allan would have an advantage because he liked to race in the rain.

With riders slipping and sliding off, the race was wild to say the least, Allan was battling in the top ten when he came together with other riders and damaged the fairing, he came past the pit box on the straightaway with the fairing flapping.

On the next lap the fairing was gone, ripped off by Allan as he went about his race. The removal and eventual loss of the fairing cost him valuable seconds and eventually he finished 15th, scoring a solitary championship point.

We celebrated this modest but positive result later in the evening at the Gasthoff Am Reidel in Koppel. Most of the paddock goes there for drinks and weiner schnitzel, and a lot of high jinks afterwards. There was also some night life in the paddock. The restaurant stayed open late and there was always a bit of ribald action each night. The star was often Randy Mamola.

In the morning it was still raining and most of the paddock had either pulled out during the night or very early morning.

I stepped outside of the motor home and noticed that we were almost the last people in the pits. Uphill from us was a motor home belonging to a pair of Italian 125 riders, Debbia and Gramigni. Imagine my shock when I saw them go to the toilet dump lever and release all of their sewage in the paddock and it was going to arrive at our motor home in a couple of seconds. I managed to jump back inside and watched the sewage sweep past on it's way to the low side of the paddock.

When I confronted the Italian riders, they just shrugged it off, I assume they thought it was a normal procedure. After this incident we never parked anywhere near those guys again.

One week later the race at Ryjeka, Yugoslavia would prove to be one of the worst events of the year!

Yugoslavia was notorious for poor medical facilities, mediocre marshaling and a host of other issues. So bad was this event that most of the top riders made it clear that if injured seriously at this circuit, they were to be taken out of Yugoslavia for treatment immediately, not to be hospitalized under any circumstances in this country.

> **"There were to be some tragic accidents as the weekend developed. Add to this a rider strike by the whole 125 contingent. Who would ever have heard of such a thing?"**

There were to be some tragic accidents as the weekend developed. Add to this a rider strike by the whole 125 contingent. Who ever heard of such a thing?

The first of several mishaps began in practice at the first corner, where riders were pressed into the bend in a tight group and making contact with each other.

We had heard that weeks earlier in the European Championship series, a rider was killed at this very spot, so it was a known problem area, and apparently still hadn't been addressed by the organizers, the result was a pile-up in the 125 race, fortunately with no serious injuries.

Everybody got a chance to fix whatever was damaged in the pile-up, but the outcome of this delay meant the TV satellite schedule was at risk and the organizers wanted to shunt the 125 race to run after the 500cc race instead of being the first TV race of the day.

The 500's were considered the premier class in Grand prix bike racing, however while that may well be the case globally, here in the heart of Europe 125's were the top draw.

Jorge Martinez and others made their living primarily from European based sponsors, and were outraged that they were not going to be broadcast at the normal time, the result was the afore mentioned strike! And the 125 guys won the day.

My good friend from the Isle of Man, Jackie Wood had the misfortune to be the FIM Steward of this disastrous Grand Prix, he was the Clerk of the Course at the TT races for years but this was his first G.P....I felt quite sorry for him as he went from incident to incident.

Allan did not finish the race when the frame of the Garelli fractured and threw him off at high speed.

He walked away with minor cuts and bruises. I still remember the look on the faces of the Garelli crew when the bike came back to the paddock in two pieces, especially that of little Eugenio Lazzarini who was stunned in disbelief, after the elation of Austria there was utter despair all round at Garelli.

That same weekend two top riders were badly injured, the German Reinhold Roth was in a coma and would never ride again, and Frenchman Christian Sarron was severely hurt with concussion and could not race that weekend.

Allan crashed when the frame broke in Yugoslavia

We left Yugoslavia a little depressed by the carnage and utter confusion we had endured, and headed for Holland to the world famous Dutch TT at Assen, clean, friendly, efficient Holland, we could hardly wait.

Assen is known as The Cathedral to many thousands of fans, who travel from all over Europe to line the whole circuit and worship Grand Prix racing once a year at this event. The paddock is superb, paved and well equipped and is fortress-like to keep it secure from raiding fans.

The first time we visited Assen, I was asleep in the paddock and woke up at daybreak to an odd sound, it was like a constant murmuring, sort of like what one hears in a theatre just before the curtain goes up.

"The sound was coming from the fans! They had slipped into the circuit in droves during the night....

The sound was coming from the fans! They had slipped into the circuit in droves during the night....

....and were now simply chatting to each other as they staked out a spot to watch the races, by late morning there would be over 100.000 and they would be juiced up and much more vocal, if you have a Bucket List put Assen on it.

Allan Scott Racing had been to Assen many times, and as a result had lots of friends in the area. It was almost like a home away from home during the long tour with many of the G.P. entourage enjoying the lure of legal prostitution in nearby Groningen, and the nightclubs where you could buy just about anything your heart desired. We used to really enjoy the annual visit to this place of rest and relaxation, just to look and watch of course? The ladies were scantily clad and usually sitting in small shop windows, some knitting and others reading or perhaps playing solitaire, smiling at the throngs of lecherous faces staring at them. The action took place on either side of a specific street, Ladies in all shapes, colors and sizes were on view and it was interesting to spot which of our more prominent colleagues were joining in the fun.

Assen was not one of Allan's better circuits and I recollect Wayne Rainey trying to give him pointers on how to approach this circuit, a place where smoothness pays off. It would not matter because Allan didn't qualify. The Garelli was back to square one again. It was another trip back to the dyno in Monticello for Jan Thiel and the crew.

Our next round on the calendar was the Belgian Grand Prix at Spa-Francorchamps in the Ardenne, a beautiful circuit that has been around for many years. This is a circuit that Allan really liked and had always lapped this circuit in the top ten, in fact he finished 6th here in 1988.

Alas, the Garelli was still way down on power and as a result, Allan did not qualify again. We were beginning to feel the doom and gloom pervading the crew and for Dani especially, it was very hard to conceal the despair. I truly felt their pain and I was nursing that same despair for Allan, who was used to dicing with the best of them, but who now had begun to show that he was despondent about the whole programme. We were of course thinking back to the day we made this contract and remembering how we could have made a terrible mistake.

We left Belgium and made our way to Le Mans for the French Grand Prix. Maybe our luck would change in France. Little

did I know that this would be Allan's last ride on a Garelli. In actuality, he was about to become the last factory rider of this once most prestigious, all conquering racing manufacturer.

In the paddock at Le Mans we located the Garelli team tent and the crew. Allan got the usual briefing about any changes made to the bike and he commenced the practice routine. Allan knew the Bugatti circuit well and the team was hoping for a good performance. Alas it was quite obvious by the stopwatch times that the bike was not up to par once again.

Dani called me into the motor home for what I assumed was payment of expenses, which he always took care of at each race, I had my receipts and documents in order and turned them over to him as usual.

"He paid me in cash and then told me that Garelli had had enough and did not want to continue with this hopeless season."

He paid me in cash and then told me that Garelli had had enough and did not want to continue with this hopeless season.

We both looked at each other and sighed. I feel it was a sigh of relief that it had come to an end. Now we had to sort out the problems facing us for the remainder of the season.

How could Dani fulfill his contract with Garelli's sponsors who had paid for a complete season? How could Allan Scott Racing complete it's personal commitments to their sponsors?

Allan would of course complete the year aboard his Honda RS125R's. Both bikes were in London. What about the motor home leased by Garelli, was it to be returned to Milan right away?

I came up with this solution. Our Hondas' were still a basic white as were the Garelli's. What if Dani spoke to his various sponsors and offered to carry their logos on the two Honda machines for the remainder of the season?

He felt that he could sell this programme. Allan Scott Racing would retain the use of the motor home and travel expenses to complete the year of racing.

Even more logical was the fact that we were headed back to the U.K. immediately after this event, and would simply collect the Hondas' in London, Dani would then arrange to have all the decals and logs delivered to the British Grand Prix at Donington Park, and we would campaign on behalf of Garelli's sponsors for the remainder of 1990..

This was acceptable to the Garelli sponsors and we all shook hands. It was the end of Garelli for the rest of season 1990, and very likely the end of the Garelli dynasty. I am sure that Dani Agrati was devastated by his decision to call it a day.

Author David Scott, Allan and Jeff showing the Garelli sponsor logos on the Honda for the Swedish TT.

Affixed with the Garelli sponsor logos, Allan rode his Honda in the Swedish TT.

Allan, Jeff and I were saddened by the Garelli season ending like this. We too were proud to have been a part of this historic year, in the knowledge that Allan gave it his best and would join the ranks of all previous Garelli riders.

We always knew that this would be a one year contract, especially if Allan had managed to return Garelli to the podium once again, there would have been no shortage of top Italian riders eager to ride this bike once more.

Now we were off to our home G.P. at Donington, because my wife Jean and our four young kids had emigrated from Scotland to California in 1967, and Allan was of course born in Scotland, therefore we had many family and friends to greet us in the U.K. We only hoped that all the fellow riders who had begged for our passes at all of their home races this year, would now honor the deal we made, which was to give us all their passes for our families when we got to the British Grand Prix. It turned out that only one rider failed to come through as agreed, Fausto Ricci.

The paddock pass issue was important, not only because many family members were coming from Scotland to cheer for Allan at Donington, but Allan's mother (my wife Jean) was joining us all the way from San Francisco, we would need every pass we could get.

When practice began at Donington and Allan immediately went on to the leader board, this drove home how poor the Garelli had been. Dani was there and had to concede that Allan had had his work cut out riding the Garelli, Allan finally qualified in 14th less than 1.5 seconds slower than the pole sitter German Stefan Prein, Allan retired the Honda on lap 4 with gear shift problems.

Still, Allan was elated to be back on a competitive bike again, and was confident that he would do well at Anderstorp in Sweden, the next 125 round.

"Dani Agrati was now a true believer. He had just witnessed Allan mixing it up with the top ten contenders. Now he realized just how awful the 1990 Garelli had been."

Dani Agrati was now a true believer. He had just witnessed Allan mixing it with the top ten contenders. Now he realized just how awful the 1990 Garelli had been.

We set off on the long journey to Sweden, mostly via several ferry crossings, but it was quite good fun and a chance to relax for a spell with the whole racing contingent. It was a great big party actually!

Allan qualified in 15th place and was pleased to be on the third row of the grid.

The race was fast and furious as usual, but it was terrific to see Allan up there amongst the leaders once more. Four laps into the race however, the engine developed a problem and he had to retire.

As we headed back to the U.K, we noticed that the motor home gearbox had started to make slight clicking sounds, especially in second gear. On arrival in England we stopped at a Ford dealer in Dover and had them lisren to the transmission noise, draining the gear oil unfortunately produced a solitary gear tooth and metallic particles. This was very bad news, but the technician suggested replacing the recommended oil with a thicker viscosity.

When we explained that we still had to go to Czechoslovakia and Hungary, plus drive the vehicle back to Milan, the Service manager grinned and said…Good luck lads!

After a meeting of the minds with Allan and Jeff, we decided to take the bikes back to our base in

Wallington. Czecho was out of the question, but we might make it to Hungary and back to Milan if we stayed out of second gear and drove conservatively.

At the same time, Jeff said he would like to head back to San Francisco. The last race in Europe in Hungary would not be aboard our bikes anyway, so he was free to go.

"We had been approached by MotoMorini to ride a prototype 125 in Hungary earlier, and Allan agreed to the one-time deal with obvious reservations!"

We had been approached by MotoMorini to ride a prototype 125 in Hungary earlier, and Allan agreed to the one time deal with obvious reservations.

This pretty much sums up the Garelli racing story.... however the motor home finally blew the ailing transmission in Vienna en route to the Hungarian Grand Prix, and we had to have it towed into a local Austrian Ford dealership.

Sadly, the extended mechanical warranty Dani had purchased proved to be invalid outside of Italy, and I heard much later that the motor home eventually had to be brought back to Milan on a flat bed truck to be repaired, extremely bad luck and very costly for Garelli.

By the way, while the vehicle was at the Viennese Ford dealership, and Allan and I were in Hungary, it was ransacked and all of our belongings stolen, the Ford people would not assume any responsibility for the theft.

Allan and I took the famous Orient Express from Vienna to Budapest to get to the Hungaroring. This was not the luxurious train that Agatha Christie made famous, just a regular crowded, dirty train service with toilets that simply dumped straight on to the tracks when it occasionally flushed.

The ***Morini*** team knew that Allan would only ride their prototype in Hungary if it was professionally prepared, and he said he would decide when he met the bike. It was indeed beautifully prepped and the Morini guys also told us that Loris Reggiani was somewhat involved in this project back in Bologna, Italy. Loris was highly respected by everyone, so Allan took the bike out in practice and immediately qualified it!

It was a bit underpowered however and only lasted 11 laps!

Regardless, the small group of technicians were quite pleased with the overall result. They had a little party afterwards and then gave us the very modest fee agreed upon, but only after a desperate round-up of cash from each of them.

Only one more Grand Prix remained, Australia.

We returned to Monticello for our final time to visit the Garelli factory and wind up our contract, traveling back to Milan from Vienna by train and were met by Dani Agrati.

Our final business was concluded amicably, Garelli fulfilling all of the agreed financial terms. Dani then delivered Allan and I to Milan's Linate airport for the short flight back to London.

Back at the base in Wallington at the home of our good friends Paul and Deborah Stow, we began to plan our eventual return to San Francisco.

Our bikes and baggage had to be crated correctly for shipment by sea back to Oakland, California. With help from Paul we found crates to do the job. All that was needed was to have the shipping company come and pick up the cargo.

There was still the Australian Grand Prix of course!

I had spoken with the Italian **Team Rumi** manager in Hungary, and he said that he was upset with his current rider, the Finnish girl Taru Rinne.

He felt that Taru was unlikely to attend the Australian race, if in fact this happened, would Allan take over the ride?

I called Team Rumi from Wallington and they confirmed that she would not ride in Australia, so Allan would be the rider and we made the required change with the organizers I.R.T.A.

Team Rumi would fly out from their base in Bergamo via Milan, and we would fly out from London but return to San Francisco directly after the race, season over!

Allan had trouble adapting to the Taru Rinne set up, and fell off in the race sustaining severe damage to his little finger.

"The medical center doctor sent for me to review the damage to Allen's finger, recommending amputation. I said, 'absolutely not'".

The medical center doctor sent for me to review the damage to Allen's finger, recommending amputation. I said, "absolutely not".

I asked them to do a really good job of dressing and bandaging the hand, we were flying home the next day and I assured them that he would have it seen to in San Francisco. They reluctantly agreed to release him……***now the 1990 season was really and truly over, amen!***

Allan and our German representative Rolf Korrmann on the grid at the Hungaroring in Budapest Hungary.

One final explanation is in order: You will have noticed that Allan's number changed from 10 in mid-season to number 9. This came about when Spanish rider Jorge Martinez, the actual owner of number 9, always preferred the number 5 throughout his career. However, the number 5 was already in use by Fausto Gresini, so he chose to ride with 55 and agreed that we could use the vacant number 9. This had something to do with superstition I believe.

Allan's final race of 1990 was in Australia for Team Rumi

Team Rumi Team Manager, Allan and Dave "Scotty" Scott.

But just as Allan Scott had discovered in 1990, when once again aboard a really good bike, he instantly rejoined the top group of competitors and recovered rapidly from the disasterous and confidence draining gamble we made with Garelli.....and to think that I had tried to own a Garelli!

We would just like to say to Garelli Thanks for the memories, Dani.

There is also a very remarkable comparison in this Garelli story, in today's World Grand Prix racing, now known as MotoGP, a very similar scenario has just emerged.

Two seasons ago in 2010, Valentino Rossi left his tried and very successful Yamaha ride, to take on the challenge of taming the least rider friendly Italian built Ducati, he took along his famous crew chief Jeremy Burgess, confident that between them they would sort out this tricky bike. You would be correct to think that this was probably a perfect marriage. The project was a complete failure and Valentino returned to Yamaha in 2013.

Allan #44 Rainey Team Yamaha and team mate Kenny Roberts Jr on the outside lead a WERA race in 1992.

Allan and multi-time World Champion Kenny Roberts Sr. confer.

Allan on the Harris 500cc Yamaha #44.

Epilogue

At the end of the 1990 season we returned home to regroup, and we all literally took the 1991 season off!

Allan had had an offer from World Champion Wayne Rainey to partner young Kenny Roberts Junior in a new team aboard 250cc Yamahas, and was thinking it over.

Allan and Kenny Roberts Jr.

It was attractive to Allan, and he eventually accepted the deal, which was to race in the 1992 WERA series all across the USA…..in which he finished in joint second place on points with KRJR, but Allan had the most wins!

I had two new 125's ordered for the 1991 season, and couldn't cancel the order, plus I had a Mercedes transporter/motorhome parked in London.

My feeling was that I had no place in the Rainey team set-up. I believed that Allan would greatly benefit from the combined experience and professionalism of Wayne and Kenny Robetrs Sr. I was certain my presence would have been a distraction.

I remember speaking with Wayne at the first joint test session at Laguna Seca. We were eating fajitas during a lunch break BBQ.

Son and dad at Wayne Rainey's test session and BBQ at Laguna Seca in early 1991.

He was telling me that he was a bit concerned about Allan falling off during the initial tests. I think Allan may have dropped the bike three times with minor damage to either party.

I said that he had better get used to fall offs. Allan was a 125 rider, the most ferocious class in World Grand Prix, and we were quite used to this!

When we worked with Allan in this extremely competitive class, I always told Allan to just get out there and give it your all son. Don't think about crashing. We can fix any damage if you fall off. I told Allan that we knew that he was exploring the absolute limit when a fall happens. I knew he was trying his best to search for that maximum limit.

Wayne was absolutely horrified, and stated categorically that this mentality would not be acceptable in his team, because we don't fall off in the Roberts/Rainey teams.

I believe that I stated that everyone has to fall off sometime, and that in my experience, it usually meant that a non-falling rider was in for a whopper when they inevitably did fall off!

That was when I realized that I would not be an asset to Allan in his new team.

Jean and I talked about the coming year without Allan around. She had been told of a possible layoff at work, so between us we decided to go to Europe anyway, at least to clear up Allan Scott Racing affairs over there.

I had to sell these two new 125 Hondas here in California first. I then put out a press release that Allan was now a Team Rainey member, but Allan Scott Racing was still in business, and would entertain the management of any eligible FIM approved 125 rider who aspired to race in Europe, but was not sure how to go about it.

Philip Unhola of Canada was an applicant. His federation, CMA, had approved him, and the FIM concurred. We would agree to transport him and his Honda up until the German Grand Prix at Hockenheim. If Philip had not yet qualified by then, I would withdraw his entry and return him and his bike to London for shipment back to Canada. Philip was a great guy, but not up to the W.G.P. level,. Sadly he went home without qualifying once!

Jean and I continued our stay in Europe, getting frequent paddock updates from Kenny Roberts and Wayne Rainey on the progress of Allan and Kenny Jr., who were slugging it out back in the U.S. WERA series.

We came home in August after selling our assets in Europe. Thankfully Allan had been paying the mortgage while we were away. It sure was nice to be home at last.

Jean went back to work almost immediately. However, I was not keen to go back to the regimentation of the car business. I had been away too long, operating with complete freedom, and answering to no one. What on earth was I suited to now?

I finally went to work for a large national printing company as a courier, driving a company car, delivering computer discs and advertising materiel, all over the San Francisco area. I operated remotely from home, responding to head office assignments delivered by phone and fax. The perfect job for a guy like me!

Allan had one more grand prix outing in 1993 aboard a 500cc Harris Yamaha This was a three race bought ride, arranged and paid for by me, brokered through my Isle of Man friend Peter Padgett. I felt that Allan could do well and deserved a shot.

This was one time when I completely reversed my advice to Allan. I had been warned by Padgett that I would be responsible for any crash damage incurred. For example, a set of new front forks cost 12.000 British pounds, roughly $19.000 he told me!

It was a miserable thought for Allan, that he might cost us a small fortune if he dropped the bike. As a result we never got to see the real Allan Scott at work, because of this threat hanging over him.

Life returned to normal eventually back in California. Jean and I retired and I became absorbed in the Caledonian Club of San Francisco, running the Press room for several years at the annual Scottish Gathering and Games held in Pleasanton, California (the largest in the world). I would later become 1st Chieftain for two years, and then rise to become the Chief of this 148 years old organization in 2010 and 2011.

I first made contact with the Caledonian Club in 1984 when Allan Scott Racing purchased a booth at the annual Scottish Games when they were held in Santa Rosa, California, to hopefully raise funds and campaign our racing team, which was of course founded by Jean and I, two full blown Scottish emigrants. We did very well with this fund raiser. Many Scots contributed to our effort, including the Caledonian Club.

Allan went back to school and studied communications, and now works for a national communications company, where he is a fiber optics engineering specialist, proving that there really is life after racing!

What a fabulous adventure life has been, I wouldn't have missed it for the world.

www.ingramcontent.com/pod-product-compliance
Lightning Source LLC
Chambersburg PA
CBHW081237170426
43198CB00017B/2789